MY PRIDE

MY PRIDE

Mastering Life's Daily Performance

by Alton Fitzgerald White
with Michael Lassell

EDITIONS

Los Angeles • New York

For information address Disney Editions, 1101 Flower Street, Glendale, California 91201.
Printed in the United States of America
Reinforced binding

First Hardcover Edition, November 2017
10 9 8 7 6 5 4 3 2 1
FAC-020093-17265

ISBN 978-1-4847-8040-4

Cover design by Winnie Ho

Book design and composition by Arlene Schleifer Goldberg

SUSTAINABLE FORESTRY INITIATIVE   Certified Sourcing
www.sfiprogram.org
SFI-00993

THIS LABEL APPLIES TO TEXT STOCK

THIS BOOK IS DEDICATED TO MY SIBLINGS, GLORIA, JIMMY, MARCIA, PAULA, ANNA, AND DARLENE; AND TO MY FATHER, PAUL W. WHITE, WHO WALKS WITH ME AND GUIDES ME IN SPIRIT EVERY DAY OF MY LIFE; AND MOSTLY TO MY GREATEST FAN, MY MUMMY-WUMMY, MARIETTA WHITE, WITH MORE GRATITUDE THAN ANY SON COULD EVER EXPRESS TO HIS MOTHER.

Contents

Introduction Thomas Schumacher xi

Foreword By Way of Introduction xv

Chapter 1 King of My World 3

Chapter 2 When You Wish Upon a Star,
Prepare to Work Your Tail Off! 17

Chapter 3 Rough Beginnings 29

Chapter 4 Michael Jackson and the Buffer Closet 49

Chapter 5 Educating Alton 63

Chapter 6 We the Peoples 85

Chapter 7 The Birth of an Actor 105

Chapter 8 To College and Beyond 125

Chapter 9 My Kind of Town, Chicago Is! 151

Chapter 10 My First Bite of the Big Apple 181

Chapter 11 *Ragtime* 211

Chapter 12 My *Lion King* 239

Chapter 13 New Ways to Roar . . . and Purr 275

MY PRIDE

Introduction

I have known Alton Fitzgerald White for more than fifteen years—and when I think of him, my first reaction is to smile. His giant talent, kindness, and compassion are his signatures. And beneath all of that is a man of extraordinary dignity.

When Alton first told me that he wanted to write a book about his experiences on the stage, I immediately thought it was a sensational idea. What I could not have anticipated was that it would simultaneously be a memoir, a "how to," a chronicle of our time, and a workbook for young artists.

Often we think the primary occupation of the actor is the complex and frequently heartbreaking task of auditioning, and (if lucky) "getting a gig." But in this insightful, personal, and clear-eyed book, Alton not only tells us about his beginnings, but also about the *life* of the actor—and what goes in to *keeping* a job. His advice and point of view are essential reading.

Talk about keeping a job, Alton's more than four thousand performances as Mufasa in Julie Taymor's landmark production of *The Lion King* is hardly rivaled by other stage actors. It is nothing short of astounding how many times he has played our King, and become the spiritual leader of the production.

Alton's well-documented experiences facing cultural bias as a black man living in contemporary Washington, DC, and particularly in New York City, which ironically occurred when he was perfoming as Coalhouse Walker Jr. in *Ragtime*, are both shattering and inspiring. Alton is not afraid to share with readers this saga and describe the part it played in shaping his art.

Alton selflessly reveals his story, his heart, and his expansive performance history to bring readers into his world and acquaint them with the nuances and facets of that world as an example, a guide, and an analysis—offering a caveat about exploring a career in the complex culture of the stage.

By sharing his story, Alton is certainly offering insight into his life and work. But much more importantly, he is opening doors—particularly for young actors of color for whom it is imperative that we build a home onstage and on the screen.

As a young man with dreams of working in the theater, there were very few (if any) deeply personal books that I could turn to for an honest assessment of a career in this profession, and of the challenges every actor faces, as well as guidance on how to get there.

Blessedly, Alton Fitzgerald White has also filled this void with his book—and brought so much more to it. The result is a one-of-a-kind view on the state of the twenty-first century American theater, from a perspective only Alton Fitzgerald White could offer.

Thomas Schumacher
Producer and President, Disney Theatrical Group

Foreword

BY WAY OF
INTRODUCTION

Your work is going to fill a large part of your life, and the only way to be truly satisfied is to do what you believe is great work. And the only way to do great work is to love what you do. If you haven't found it yet, keep looking. Don't settle. As with all matters of the heart, you'll know when you find it.
—Steve Jobs, cofounder and CEO of Apple, Inc.

My name is Alton Fitzgerald White, and I am an actor. I do some other things, too, of course, but "actor and singer" pretty much sums up my professional life. Until recently you could have seen me on Broadway playing King Mufasa in *The Lion King*, the megahit stage musical based on Disney's 1994 animated blockbuster film. My thirteen-year tenure with *The Lion King* in New York, Las Vegas, and on tour around the United States has been without a doubt the highlight of my thirty-year career—at least so far! By the time I left the show on July 5, 2015, I had performed the role 4,308 times. It's not a world record, but I am extremely proud of my longevity and even prouder of the work I did at every one of those 4,308 shows.

As an actor, and as a man, I have learned a lot over the years—principles that I use to guide my life, practices that help keep me going no matter how tough things get, and insights into ways of enriching both my life and career. I may not be as wise as Mufasa, arguably Disney's wisest father, but I think there are things I have learned that might interest and even help others—not just fellow actors and singers, fellow performers, and fellow artists, but everyone. Because the principles, practices, and insights that inform my life are, I believe, universal.

As the always-insightful William Shakespeare wrote in *As You Like It,* "All the world's a stage," and in many ways, it certainly is. For one thing, I think it's safe to say that most of us seek applause—the validation that we have done well—both from our loved ones and colleagues and from the greater community. And we hope that our hard work and commitment will earn us the accolades we seek and the benefits of success. There is nothing more natural than wanting recognition for our efforts in both our careers and in our personal lives.

Now, your personal stage may be a boardroom or

a classroom, or at the head of a household, or along an assembly line. Regardless, in every scenario, that desire to succeed and be recognized remains the same. My stage of choice has been the performing arts, and my life—which did not have the most auspicious beginning—has been made richer and fuller by the extraordinary, satisfying, and sometimes-glamorous life I have led. But all lives, no matter the professional and personal choices, share certain challenges that are identical for everyone. The aspiration to achieve and maintain consistent excellence and to reap the fruits of our labor is universal.

As an actor, I have worked consistently for more than thirty years in a notoriously difficult arena, with more than twenty of those years on Broadway. I may not be a household name, but thankfully I am well-known in the rarefied world of the theater, thanks to having played leading roles in some major hits—shows that were socially meaningful as well as popular, including *Ragtime*, *Miss Saigon*, *The Color Purple*, and, of course, *The Lion King*. But I would never have been able to accomplish any of this without the lessons I learned along the way— lessons that, once learned, became the motivators for even greater professional and personal aspiration, achievement, and satisfaction.

One of those lessons is how important it is to balance the passion for what you do with restorative self-nurturing. We hear a great deal about being passionate in our work, about choosing our passion and following our bliss. But passion alone can lead to burning out if it is not accompanied by some understanding of the way our passion functions, and of what we must do to keep our passions healthy and focused. Unfocused passion can be exhausting and destructive, and can actually hinder rather than help us.

My Pride is an attempt to share what I hope is the wisdom that I have gained by performing—and by performing I don't just mean acting or singing on a stage or screen. I mean performing the service of my craft to benefit others, as well as myself. These are the lessons, precious to me, that I began to learn while navigating my particular American childhood. As a young boy of color being raised in public housing, I felt that very little was expected of me. I had to learn to raise my own expectations and to succeed on terms that helped me heal myself and become something much more than what others expected of me.

My journey has been a rich adventure, full of triumphant highs—and intense challenges. The rewards have been great, but so have the sacrifices. The accomplishments of living our lives to the fullest can be most gratifying, but they are sometimes hard-won and come at a cost. I believe that the greatest spiritual gifts come from enduring the most challenging circumstances, and that no one is exempt. We must all go through the process in our own way. How we perceive the difficulties and what we do to resolve them define who we really are.

My experiences have taught me the importance of redefining service, which is one of the best ways we can actually motivate ourselves in periods of boredom, doubt, or fatigue. The objective of this book is to inspire and encourage you with what I have discovered about tapping into instinct, devotion, planning, training, investing, valuing what you have to offer, and fostering the emotional and physical stamina necessary to pursue and sustain a life and career of excellence on your personal life's stage and even beyond, to places you never thought possible.

Capabilities and talents in this world are abundant and diverse. But passion for what you do is not enough. You also need the passion to commit yourself to a kind of physical, mental, emotional, and spiritual fitness in order to excel. Many strive, but only those who dedicate themselves to consistent and continued excellence endure and transcend.

My Pride is not a program. It isn't a rule book or a catechism. My hope is that you'll see it as a gift. It comes from my heart, because I believe in what it says. I believe that my experiences can be helpful to anyone in any walk of life. If you agree, if any of it works for you, I will be thrilled—but I won't be surprised.

My hope, my *prayer*, is that this book will inspire and motivate you to identify and nurture qualities in yourself that will help make your abundant dreams come true *on your own terms*. We have been taught by society to think that "the pot of gold at the end of the rainbow" is money and fame, but the authentic, lasting prize is an acknowledgment of success that is already within you. The knowledge that you have done your very best without having to rely predominantly on outside validation is a powerful asset. Only you can validate yourself, and that validation is *enough*! That powerful feeling is *your* pride. Once you learn to tap into that inner resource, your ultimate success is sure to follow.

Alton Fitzgerald White
New York City
2017

Chapter 1

KING OF MY WORLD

I'm not going to start my story from the beginning (for the early chapters of my life were not nearly as joyful as those of my present and recent past). Instead, I want to begin with one of the best days of my life, a day that symbolizes for me the success that my life has been—the day I performed the role of King Mufasa in Disney's *The Lion King* for the four thousandth time.

Later I'll tell you about my challenging formative years, but first I want to offer up a view at what my life in art looks like when everything is aligned, when my life and career are in balance and harmony. I have a lot of days like that, actually, but some are more perfect than others.

The Lion King opened on Broadway in 1997. I joined the "family," as we say, for the Gazelle Tour, the original *Lion King* tour of the United States. My very first night, which was at the Denver Center for the Performing Arts, was on April 21, 2002. I traveled with that tour to major cities across the country and was then asked to join the Broadway cast. When *The Lion King* began its residency at the Mandalay Bay Resort in Las Vegas, I was with the original company, after which I moved back to Broadway.

Mile after mile, show after show, my number of performances as King Mufasa was slowly but surely growing. Still, I wasn't keeping track of how many times I had suited up and gone out there onstage as the King of Pride Rock.

One day back in 2014, when I was doing some press for *The Lion King*, Dennis Crowley, Disney Theatrical Group's public relations chief (and a friend since *Miss Saigon* in 2001), was there to oversee the process. We were reminiscing about how lucky we both felt to still be doing what we loved to do. Then, out of nowhere, he asked me if I knew the number of shows I'd done as King Mufasa. I had no idea! My main focus had been on gratitude for being a working actor and doing the best I could at every show. After doing some math, we approximated that I was at or very near four thousand. Dennis and I were both amazed by the number. He noted that Carol Channing in *Hello, Dolly!* and Yul Brynner in *The King and I* were two of the very few actors who'd had that kind of longevity playing the same character, and Dennis encouraged me to acknowledge it in some way.

It turned out that my four thousandth performance was to be on Saturday, August 23, 2014, the evening of a hectic two-show day at the Minskoff Theatre, one of the few Broadway theaters that is actually *on* Broadway. It would be a perfect time for me to mark what I considered a proud moment and a significant achievement.

That morning, I woke earlier than usual for a matinee day in order to prepare for a special recording session for a lovely woman named Dodie Petit. Dodie's late husband, the actor Kevin Gray, was a well-loved, well-known Broadway leading light who died very suddenly of a heart attack on February 11, 2013, at the age of fifty-five. Kevin's unforeseen death shocked and saddened the theater community in New York and beyond. Kevin and I had both appeared in *Miss Saigon*, but not at the same time, and I never had the pleasure of working with him, or even meeting him. I did know that he was highly regarded not only for his versatile talent, but also for his wonderful personality and great kindness.

As a tribute to his memory, Dodie decided to produce an album of inspirational songs performed by many of Broadway's best voices. It would be a fund-raising CD benefiting two endowed scholarships in Kevin's name—one for the Hartt School at the University of Hartford (in Connecticut), where he'd been an associate professor, and the other for Duke University (in Durham, North Carolina), his alma mater. When Dodie contacted me and asked if I'd sing "They Live in You" from *The Lion King* on the CD, I agreed immediately. It is no small testament to Kevin that Disney, which rarely allows anyone outside the company to record its music, would allow the song to be used, and I felt honored to be asked to sing it.

"They Live in You" is a stunning, transformative, mid-tempo ballad, as we say in the trade, with music by South African musician Lebo M. and lyrics by Lebo, Mark Mancina, and Jay Rifkin. Mufasa sings "They Live in You" to Young Simba after the cub asks his dad if they will always be together. In the song, Mufasa assures his son that although he will physically die someday, his spirit and the spirits of all those who have gone before him will be with Simba and live in him forever.

Later, when Young Simba matures into Adult Simba (as the two characters are officially called), and he is ready to go deeper into his own heroic journey of discovery, he sings an up-tempo variation of that same song titled "*He* Lives in You." In the song, Simba exclaims that, with his father's spirit inside him, he is ready to become a man, to return home, and to take his rightful place as king.

The idea for the CD was to put the two versions together, beginning with Mufasa's version and then having it build triumphantly into Adult Simba's take. Even better, I would be recording the song with the first Adult Simba that I'd ever worked with, my good buddy Josh Tower. Josh and I opened the Gazelle Tour of *The Lion*

King back in 2002 and shared a dressing room in the theaters of almost every city we played. We had also shared a stage in *Ragtime* many years before.

At a time when I had no knowledge of my four thousandth performance as King Mufasa approaching, Dodie chose the morning of August 23 as my recording date for the CD. It felt like divine order that the session would fall on the same day that I had chosen to formally acknowledge my own personal milestone. It was the perfect way for me to begin what was to be an unforgettable day. Recording the song for a charitable cause provided a wonderful opportunity for me to be of service with my time and talent and to thank the universe for the many gifts I've been given.

Two-show days are very demanding. The discipline, stamina, and focus required to do a single show is tough, and *more* than twice the energy is needed for a double-header. Pacing yourself is a must. On a regular two-performance day, I try to sleep until at least 10:00 A.M. and then do my morning routine, adding a trip to the gym for a forty-five-minute workout before I go to the theater for the matinee. That particular morning, my alarm went off at an excruciating 7:00 A.M., about five hours after I'd gotten to sleep (since I had performed the night before). Following the order of my morning rituals, I got up and stretched a little while enjoying the morning stillness. I showered as the coffee maker worked its fragrant magic. Next, I got dressed, drank coffee, scarfed down some strawberry yogurt, did vocal exercises for about a half hour, and left at about 8:15.

The recording session was to start at eleven, which gave me about an hour to take care of vital business regarding my evening's celebration. I had planned the festivities for the intermission of the evening performance. One of the key ingredients for my little party was cake. Not just any cake, but chocolate cake. Not just any chocolate cake, but chocolate cake from the Little Pie Company on Forty-Third Street, which is at the western fringe of the Theater District. It is *the best* chocolate cake in New York City, with a perfect flaky, moist texture that's an exquisite combination of bitter and sweet. And the frosting? OMG!—rich, thick, and bittersweet chocolaty. Just *perfect*. I'd ordered a half sheet, double layer, enough to feed fifty comfortably.

A couple of weeks before my big day, I sent an informal e-vite to some folks at the Disney Theatrical office and to the cast and crew. I wrote that if they happened to be in or near the theater at intermission during the show that Saturday evening, to please feel free to come by my dressing room for the best chocolate cake in the city, a glass of sparkling cider, and fresh strawberries.

I was very blessed to have one of only a few dressing rooms on all of Broadway that has a window! The view was of Forty-Fifth Street, with a nice sliver of Broadway and the bright lights of Times Square.

Since I spent so much of my time there, I had it set up like a studio apartment, with a couch, extra chairs, and a fridge. Most of the company birthdays, happy trails fare-wells, and so forth are held in a very narrow, somewhat crowded hallway at the Minskoff. But I wanted a more personal, more intimate celebration, so I scheduled it to be held in my dressing room.

The Little Pie Company was opening at ten, and I was the first customer of the day, eagerly waiting by 9:50.

The cake looked and smelled amazing. The words 4,000TH PERFORMANCE AS KING MUFASA were spelled out in red. I couldn't believe it when I saw that number spelled out in the icing. *Four thousand?* It still didn't seem possible. They boxed it up for me and I *very carefully* walked it over to the theater.

From there it was just a few blocks up to Seventh Avenue and Forty-Ninth Street to the recording studio. I arrived at 10:45 and finally got to meet Dodie in person; she's a lovely and passionate woman. It was also great to see my friend Josh again. He had just recently taken over the role of Berry Gordy Jr. in *Motown* on Broadway, and his wife had very recently delivered their second child—on his opening night of the show!

We rehearsed the new arrangement of the song. We sang through the track a couple of times and then went into the sound booth, put on our headphones, and began recording. After doing about five or six takes, Dodie and the sound engineer called Josh and me out to listen to what we'd recorded. They were pleased with what they heard, and after less than an hour, we called it a wrap.

This left me the perfect amount of time to run to a nearby grocery store to grab utensils, napkins, and a few bottles of sparkling cider, along with the promised fresh strawberries to go with the cake.

Then the surprises started.

When I got back to the Minskoff, there was a beautiful flower arrangement waiting for me. When I opened the card to see who sent it, my mouth dropped open. It read: "Congratulations! Thank You for 4,000 Amazing Performances!" The flowers were from Thomas Schumacher, president of Disney Theatrical Group, and Anne Quart, producer/general manager, and the card was signed by both of them. I was sincerely taken aback. I had no idea that the company would do anything to recognize the day, and I honestly did not expect anything from them. Disney Theatrical Group is a huge international company, and its two top executives are extraordinarily busy. The flowers and note were gorgeous and left me stunned.

When I turned on my computer, there were dozens of social media posts from friends and family all over the world congratulating me. All the theater websites—Playbill.com, Theatermania.com, Broadwayworld.com—and newspapers as far away as the *Los Angeles Times* had announcements and articles about me and my milestone performance. When I pulled out my phone to share this with my mother, my number one cheerleader, my phone was already full of congratulatory messages and texts.

After the matinee, the theater's doorman called and said that I had a guest waiting for me. I wasn't expecting anyone, but my best friend, Rashid Davis, had surprised me and come to the matinee. He'd planned to attend my four thousandth performance that evening, but the show was already completely sold out. He is the only person I know whose schedule is as packed as mine, so I was really thrilled that he made the effort to surprise me.

When I walked through the stage door for the evening performance, I was floored by one of the largest, most beautiful flower arrangements I'd ever seen. It was from my family, with a note saying how proud of me they were for persistently pursuing my dreams and reaching my record-breaking performance. A little later, with a mere 3,999 performances as Mufasa under my belt, I was sitting in my dressing room in costume and about to go to the stage for the "places" call when there was a knock on my door. Chris Recker, one of our company managers, had come to congratulate me. Then he handed me a stack of gold papers. He said that Disney had stuffed the evening's playbills with them and that Disney thought that I might like to have some of them for myself. Printed on each of the papers in bold type was CONGRATULATIONS TO ALTON FITZGERALD WHITE ON HIS 4000TH PERFORMANCE AS MUFASA IN DISNEY'S THE LION KING! I was completely blown away!!! The thought that they had taken the time to design it, print it, and distribute it nearly took my breath away.

The evening's performance was a magical one, and singing Mufasa's "They Live in You" took on deeper meaning, especially the lyrics "They live in you, they live in me, they're watching over everything we see" and "In your reflection, they live in you." It reminded me of all the many performers of color who had come before me and had not been afforded the opportunity to ever make it to Broadway, much less achieve a milestone like this in one of theater's greatest all-time hits. This landmark performance of mine was in honor of them and the courageous trail that they blazed to make something like this at all possible for me.

During that show, my entire performance took me back to being a kid and watching, learning, and getting inspiration from my favorite television stars who kept me company when I had no friends of my own. This event was an offering of my gratitude to all of them and their memory.

At intermission, folks from the cast, crew, and orchestra gathered in my room to celebrate with "Celebration," one of my favorite Madonna songs, blasting in the background. I got hugs, handshakes, and kisses galore, and I received them all wholeheartedly! We toasted with our glasses of sparkling cider, and I personally sliced a wedge of cake for every one of my guests so that they knew that the king himself was serving them.

After the show, I stopped by the stage door, as usual, to sign autographs and take pictures with fans. Then I took the No. 1 subway train uptown to Columbus Circle to my favorite restaurant, The Smith, directly across from Lincoln Center. Five of my best buddies were waiting to celebrate with me. We had a fantastic meal, and the champagne flowed for the rest of the evening and into early the next morning. Just before The Smith closed, I slipped away to secretly pay the bill and treat my family of friends.

Surprising them like that was an even bigger treat for me, especially when I saw the startled looks on their faces. They would have done the very same for me, and I know for a fact that they had planned to that evening, but I got to the waiter before they did! Truly, there is nothing better than giving. It was an excellent way to end a truly excellent day.

The festivities came to a close. I couldn't stop laughing and smiling on my way home. I was *so* happy! I felt like I had won my own special Tony Award and celebrated my two favorite holidays, Thanksgiving and Christmas, all in one. What an amazing, eventful day it had been. To receive that kind of validation for my work and passion was moving almost beyond words. I was really feeling the "Circle of Life," as well as the circle of giving with gratitude.

Back home, I showered and washed off after my long

day and tried, really tried, to sleep, but I was still way too excited. I lay there in bed thinking, *How on earth did a poor black kid from the Cincinnati projects, with no musical training and an extreme lack of confidence, make it out of public housing and onto the stage of six hit Broadway shows?* And I knew in my heart that if it could happen for me, it could happen for anybody.

Somehow I can't believe there are many heights that can't be scaled by a man who knows the secret to making dreams come true. This special secret, it seems to me, can be summarized in four Cs. They are Curiosity, Confidence, Courage, Constancy, and the greatest of these is Confidence. When you believe a thing, believe it all over, implicitly and unquestioningly.

—**Walt Disney**

Chapter 2

WHEN YOU WISH UPON A STAR, PREPARE TO WORK YOUR TAIL OFF!

Life requires thorough preparation. Veneer isn't worth anything; we must disabuse ourselves of the idea that there is a short cut to achievement.

—George Washington Carver

The frenzy surrounding my four thousandth performance as Mufasa in *The Lion King* was joyfully overwhelming. I haven't ever won a performance award, but I realized through the various celebrations that I was being recognized for having achieved something that very few actors ever accomplish. This was a much better gift than any award, because its rewards would have no expiration date and the achievement was something that for me would never diminish or fade. As a personal celebration, I flew to Nevada to meditate in the mountains. While I was there, I crossed another item off my bucket list: I finally conquered my fear of heights by taking a helicopter ride down into the Grand Canyon. Then I flew home to Cincinnati, where my family threw me a huge party.

After the dust settled and the festivities died down, some unexpected and challenging emotions rose to the surface that I hadn't anticipated. There had been tons of salutations from many people, but a large number of them kept commenting on how lucky I was to have had such a long run. The latter, to me, felt like something of a backhanded compliment: those who thought I was "lucky" seemed to put most of the value on the financial aspect of my accomplishment while discounting the hard work, discipline, and sacrifice necessary to do what I did.

I have trouble with the notion of luck. Oh, of course it exists. You're walking along and find a twenty-dollar bill in the street. That's luck, mostly (although if you weren't observant, if you hadn't chosen to move left or right, you might have missed it). But are successful people primarily lucky, or is it something else? Or more? Isn't it because they . . . because *we* . . . have somehow earned our success?

I grant you that not everybody who tries to be successful succeeds, and it's not always their fault. But isn't success also in large measure earned by preparation, education, commitment, hard work, professionalism, and doing all the countless things a successful performer needs to do to maintain and expand the arena of his or her talent? Even working actors continue to take dance, voice, and acting classes. Luck is fickle—and it runs out. I don't feel "lucky" as much as I feel fortunate and grateful.

And I don't mean to be arrogant, but I feel a bit insulted when people write off my achievements as mere luck.

The more I thought about the luck vs. discipline and commitment idea, the more apparent the many sacrifices I'd made over the years became. I began meditating to specifically try to tap into what else might be under the surface, what I was not conscious of. I began to uncover other things that I'd had to deny myself to fulfill my passion for my work in the world of theater. Suddenly I began to feel the loss of all those missed family birthdays, weddings, graduations, and funerals. I looked back at all those six-day workweeks with their four- and five-performance weekends all while trying to fit my personal life into one "free" day a week.

Clearly a lot more goes into a successful life than dumb luck. And the more I began to think about it, the more I began to see that success in any field is not just about *achieving* success but maintaining it. My years in the world of musical theater would not have been possible if it had not been for many things other than luck. And this book is about some of them.

I'm going to tell my own story, because I got to where

I am one step at a time, slowly, over the course of many years. Sometimes I took a step back for every two I took forward, but with faith, instinct, focus, and perseverance, I was able to carve out a full, rich life as an adult that was beyond my wildest dreams as a kid.

Among the things we're going to consider as I tell you the story of my life in art (to borrow a phrase from the great Russian actor and director Konstantin Stanislavsky) are the following:

1. KEEP SIGHT OF YOUR DREAMS

Your dreams are yours alone. You don't have to explain them or justify them to anybody; you don't have to shrink them or adjust them *for* anybody. Sometimes you have to hold on tight, especially when the world around you is not responding, and your dreams seem to be fading—or moving further beyond reach. Patience is essential, and so is tenacity. Don't let go. Don't allow inevitable disappointments to define your present or future. Keeping your eye on the prize, no matter what happens, puts you on the course to fulfillment.

2. TRUST YOUR INSTINCTS

Your instincts also belong entirely to you. They are unique and a gift to help guide you in life. It takes some experience to identify them and even more experience to learn to trust them. A gut feeling can save your life, but you have to monitor your instincts to make sure you're heading in the right direction. Experience is really the only teacher. Eventually you'll learn the difference between instincts and what may be, especially early in life, a tantrum. The better the relationship you have with how you truly feel, the clearer the path will be to trusting what is right for you at any given moment. I had to learn that how I *feel* as my destiny unfolds is more important than what some situation looks or seems like from the outside.

3. BE RESPONSIBLE FOR YOUR ACTIONS AND CHOICES

Personal accountability is the only shortcut to healing and maturity. This is one of the most important lessons to learn in life, and the earlier you learn it the better. It is something that can easily be taught even to children. Almost nothing in your life happens without your participation. All actions have consequences, whether we see them or not. And we are responsible for what we do and the choices we make, whether it's how we treat other people or how we treat ourselves. Blaming others will not help you and may hurt you both personally and professionally. Own your behavior, mistakes included. Eventually it will be something that feels good and adds immeasurably to self-esteem.

4. DEVELOP DISCIPLINE AND A DEFINED WORK ETHIC

There are very few shortcuts to success in any field that matters. Talent and intellect are important, of course, but perfecting your technique is paramount. You will need to be ready for every opportunity. It's "Be Prepared" with a vengeance. You need training, preparation, education, discipline, and skill to be successful, especially in the performing arts. And while that may sound difficult and terribly serious, these are, in fact, tremendous gifts only you can give yourself. In any endeavor that is collaborative, your willingness to work to your full capacity all the time is one of the things that will help you and your colleagues, and will earn you respect and continued employment.

5. TAKE CARE OF YOURSELF

Your health is fundamental to your being able to function—at work and in your private life. And you need to take the responsibility to nurture yourself, especially once you're an adult. For some jobs, physical strength and stamina are necessary. But exercise and keeping fit are always vital to happiness. Keeping healthy, however, also means keeping emotionally and mentally healthy.

If you'd hire a trainer to help you work out at a gym,

why wouldn't you hire a psychological trainer to help you organize your thoughts and emotions? I believe that every person, especially every artist, no matter what field, could benefit from some form of therapy. There's no shame in seeking help to achieve greater clarity, whether it's individual analysis or some form of group experience. And don't forget to accept help that's offered by those who love you.

6. FOSTER A SENSE OF SPIRITUALITY

Spirituality, as I understand it, involves your relationship with the universe. That might mean involving yourself in a specific religion and worshipping an entity called God, but not necessarily. Establishing and nourishing a relationship with a higher source, however you define it, helps you maintain faith and optimism. My own spiritual life centers on the practice of Bikram yoga. I find it elating and inspiring, and there is no question at all in my mind that my work onstage is immeasurably better because of it. If you keep your eyes and ears—and more importantly your heart—open, you'll find a path that works best for you.

It takes a strong sense of spirituality, I think, to develop two extremely important traits at the root of success: forgiveness and gratitude. Resentments and grudges waste vital energy that can go into moving yourself forward in your life and career. Everyone makes mistakes.

Even you. And being grateful for everything life offers, even if you have worked hard for it, generates a sense of humility, however great your talents might be, that is powerfully attractive no matter what you do for a living.

7. COMMIT YOURSELF TO SERVICE

When many of us think of service, the image is of being submissive and passive; of being less than. But being "of service" is a gift, not only to others but to yourself as well. It doesn't actually mean doing anything you don't already want to do. It's all about your attitude in doing it.

As an actor, I am in service to a playwright, a director, a cast, and an audience—and doing my work with a focus on giving something to all those people makes showing up every day, no matter how I feel, far easier. Working hard does not have to seem like suffering, and motivating yourself by offering service to a cause close to your heart can reap great spiritual rewards (as well as financial success). An attitude of service is also key to the repetitive nature of so many jobs and occupations. I could never have performed the same role over four thousand times if I had been focusing on what I was getting rather than on what I was giving.

8. LEARN TO LIVE WITH REJECTION

Okay, let's just say it: nobody likes rejection. It tests everything you think about yourself. It's unavoidable, especially in the arts, but we just can't take it personally. Actors are rejected because they are shorter than the director might like, or taller. Sometimes the reasons you are rejected are far more pernicious and harder to accept. But you can't let yourself be paralyzed either by the fear of rejection or the fact of rejection. What you can do is redefine it, perceive it another way. Rejection can be a powerful teacher, a device that informs you about where you are on your journey. It can serve as an important marker for you to stay in touch with what you do well and what skills you need to work on and finesse.

9. UNDERSTAND SUCCESS

Only you can define success. And the chances are you will do that many times, if not constantly. You get to set the goals: Do you define success as achieving higher amounts of money, power, and prestige? Or is it about personal achievements, or creating something that makes the world a better place? Do you have to have the lead role? Or is being a superlative performer in a supporting part an equal achievement, if not even a greater success in your view?

10. BE IN BUSINESS

As the name suggests, even show business is a business. You do something and someone pays you. This is how you earn your living and pay for your life. It's vital to learn to manage money, but it's not always necessary to choose whatever makes the most money. Sometimes, especially in the arts, it's a good idea to take less money to do something that may be more self-fulfilling or more important to building your career. (Having some savings or investments behind you helps you make those decisions more freely.) The most important thing to remember is that what you do has value. Your talent is an asset, and your employers would not have hired you if they were not happy to have you. You don't want to behave like an entitled jerk, but don't ever sell yourself short, either.

Wherever you go, *you* go with you; and there is no greater feeling than the feeling of pride when you know that you have done the best that you can do. Perfection is unattainable, but excellence is not, and the more you maintain excellence, the greater the spiritual, personal, professional, and financial rewards will be.

And so, without further ado, I give you the early chapters of my life.

Enter young Alton, stage left.

Success is no accident. It is hard work, perseverance, learning, studying, sacrifice and most of all, love of what you are doing or learning to do.

—Pelé, soccer legend

Chapter 3

ROUGH BEGINNINGS

Every child has dreams. It doesn't matter where you come from. Your past informs the rest of your life, but you are more than where you come from. Expect more from life than other people expect from you. Hold on to your dreams, but stay open to new possibilities. Dreams can change. They can certainly expand!

I was born at General Hospital in Cincinnati to Marietta and Paul W. White at 12:15 P.M. on April 10, 1964, and given the name Alton Fitzgerald White. The Fitzgerald part came from President John Fitzgerald Kennedy, a man my mother respected enormously and who had been assassinated the previous November while she was carrying me. Alton (pronounced AL-ton, not ALL-ton) comes from my mother's grandfather, another man she deeply respected.

My great-grandfather Alto Copeland will always be a

hero and a savior to my mother. As a young girl, she faced many challenges, and her grandpa Alto encouraged her to put her energy and passion into books and stories. At his urging, she read anything and everything that she could get her hands on. He stressed to her the importance of learning and using her imagination as tools of survival and endurance. He encouraged her to continually do the best that she could at any given time and to hold her head high no matter what the obstacle or what judgment was passed on her.

He assured her that wherever she went, God was beside her with forgiveness and protection. Gratefully, my mother passed these lessons along to her children as well. Her eyes still light up when any mention of Alto Copeland is made.

When my mother suggested naming me after him, my father objected. He was probably expecting me to be Paul W. White Jr., but that was the last thing my mother wanted at the time. She didn't want me to be called *Junior* or to be constantly compared to my father, so they agreed on Alton, a name close to Alto, which spared me the burden of living completely in my great-grandfather's angelic shadow.

I was the last child of my parents, the youngest of seven in the family. At a very young age my then unwed mother gave birth to my oldest sister, Gloria, and soon after, to my one brother, Jimmy. A few years after having Gloria and Jimmy, Mama met my father, Paul Weyman

White, a World War II vet from a big family, when they both worked in the dining room of the Vernon Manor Hotel in Cincinnati. They married and had four girls. Before I was born, I am told, he would rant about how much he wished he had a son and would often complain about being the only man in a house full of females. (As far back as I can remember, my sister Gloria was out of the house, and my brother, Jimmy, never lived with us.) With my appearance, my father got his wish. His pride at finally having a son, however, did not cure him of the unfortunate disease of alcoholism.

So, I grew up in the Setty Kuhn Metropolitan Housing Projects in Cincinnati. Our building, at 3069 Mathers Street, was off Gilbert Avenue in the city's Walnut Hills neighborhood. Our two-story unit had three bedrooms and one bathroom with no shower, only a tub. My mother and father shared one of the bedrooms, and my four sisters shared the other two. I didn't have a bedroom of my own, so I took turns floating around from bed to bed . . . and I use the word *floating* advisedly.

Everyone dreaded it when it was my turn to hop in with them because I had a severe bed-wetting problem as a kid. Even after every possible precaution was taken, my "accidents," as they were called, were completely unpredictable. I learned as an adult that my bed-wetting was probably the result of traumatic encounters I had endured when I was victimized at school and around the neighborhood. But at the time, of course, I had no access to that kind of analysis.

My family and I tried everything to stop it. I wouldn't be allowed to drink anything for hours before I went to bed, and I would pray that I would not wake up in a pool of urine. I would sometimes go for weeks with everything being okay and feeling quite normal; but then, seemingly out of nowhere, I would be awakened by one of my sisters or parents and find myself in a wet bed. They would be furious. I would be half-asleep, embarrassed, and dumbfounded. I could never feel it happening and would wake up just as angry and frustrated as they were.

I know they didn't mean to, but they blamed me, as if I were doing it on purpose. It got to a point where I got tired of the shame of overhearing my sisters' arguments about who was going to have to let me sleep with them. It made me feel helpless and guilty. I dreaded going to bed, and as night approached, I would get increasingly anxious because ultimately, somebody in the house would be stuck with me and run the risk of getting soaked.

Out of frustration and shame, I came up with a solution of my own. There was a hallway that separated my parents' bedroom from the two my sisters occupied. There was a wall on one side of the corridor and a linen closet on the other. This closet was about six feet wide with four or five shelves in it. The bottom shelf was about two feet from the floor, which left me enough space to get in and out easily. There was no door on the closet, just a curtain.

I asked my mother if I could sleep there on the floor and make it my own. At first she said no, and I could tell that she felt bad that there really wasn't a room for me in the house. Even at a young age, I could sense Mama's guilt about my being the only boy and having no place of my own. I assured her that I would be fine on the floor of the closet by myself. The curtain of the closet hung just short of the floor and gave me some of the privacy I had been longing for. It made me feel like I finally had my own space. I made a pallet of blankets on the floor for my bed. Everyone thought it was odd, but we all knew that there was nowhere else for me to go, and I am sure everyone was relieved that they no longer had to deal with my bed-wetting. I was just happy to be out of everyone's way.

Now, for some reason, one of my big fantasies as a kid was to go camping. As an inner-city kid, heading out to the woods and sleeping in a tent seemed like an adventure. Having my own little spot on the floor of the closet with just enough room under the curtain to see my family walking by seemed like the same kind of adventure. All that was missing was an older brother who could share my adventures.

When I was growing up, Jimmy, a married adult, was stationed in Germany with his own family. When I was a kid, no one ever explained to me or discussed anything about Jimmy not living with us. I didn't get the full story until I was an adult. I was aware that I had a brother, but mostly in name only. I missed his presence a lot because I had to fend for myself in my mostly female world at home as well as the bullying world outside.

I vaguely remember him visiting when he was in the United States, but there was little relationship between us. Because I had always wanted an older brother who could show me the ropes and defend me against kids at school or in the neighborhood, I was always happy when he came by. And when he did, I tried to get close to him, like I thought brothers were supposed to be, but truthfully, he was foreign to me.

I was also secretly afraid of getting too attached, since I never knew when I'd see him next. Sometimes when I'd get teased, I would brag that I had a big brother, because it gave me the illusion of being protected. However, then I would feel deflated when the questions came: *Well, where is he? Why doesn't he live with you? How come we never see him? He's not here right now, so how can he do anything for you?*

I fought often when I was growing up, not because I wanted to, but because I was often in the position of having to defend myself. I hated fighting and, even as a kid, I'd wonder why things couldn't be solved by just talking and sorting things out. Unfortunately, "just talking" was not a popular form of communication in my neighborhood, especially with groups of kids who loved to see a big fight erupt. I could never understand the attraction of violence. I didn't relate to it at all, which made me even more of a target. My fights were almost always a result of being provoked by another kid's name-calling or teasing me about being a nerd, sissy, or teacher's pet, or calling out my father's drinking, which everyone in my neighborhood knew all about. Being sensitive by nature meant my feelings got hurt easily. I'd cry, which only led to more teasing. Then my anger would start to build and the next thing I knew, I'd be fighting someone.

I tried to be tougher, let the insults roll off my back, but at that age I had none of the tools I have learned in my later years to help me ignore them. Taking every word they said to heart, I felt ashamed. I was the awkward kid who was always outnumbered, the odds stacked against me because I was such a vulnerable target. When I would get picked on and needed an older sibling to help and defend me, I had only sisters to run to—and defend me they did! But I was one of the few boys in the projects who didn't have a brother, and this led to even more humiliation, both around the projects and at home, which would magnify my embarrassment.

Never did I wish more strongly that I had an older brother or strong male figure to guide me and help me navigate the constant challenges to my physical well-being, my reputation, my self-awareness, and my self-esteem. I so envied those who had brothers to teach them what it meant to be a boy. My mother and sisters were great role models, but as a result of a combination of circumstances—including limited guidance from male figures in my life at the time—I was becoming somewhat effeminate.

MENTALLY DETACHING FROM MY FAMILY

My sisters are all approximately two years apart, and they actually have fun stories to tell about my father cooking big meals for them and of the whole family doing enjoyable things together when they were little. Unfortunately, I don't have nearly as many pleasant childhood memories of him, so I could rarely share their nostalgic merriment. My sisters and I may have grown up in the same house, but we had very different experiences. Most of the powerful memories of my father from my childhood were neither pleasant nor funny. As an adult, I have developed compassion for what alcoholics go through, but as a young male child looking for his validation, his attitude toward me felt extremely personal.

Memories of being the target of one of his personal tirades in front of the whole family and no one being able to do anything to stop him still linger. My father seemed to get to do and say whatever he wanted in our house. No limits. No boundaries. No matter how nasty he got, he was always allowed to stay. Whether he verbally abused me in private, in front of the family, or in public, there never seemed to be any repercussion or punishment for him. Confusingly, this made me dislike him and envy him at the same time.

Whenever my father was home, he seemed to soak up the energy in the house. Even when he rested, the focus was on him. We'd try to guess how long he might be asleep and what kind of mood he might be in when he woke up, especially if he was coming down from a bender. In my young eyes, he always got all the vital attention. Everything seemed to revolve around him and what he needed, or what needed to be done to keep him peaceful and quiet.

I had no one to turn to when my father was out of control. My sisters had each other, and their closeness must have been beneficial when they had to endure my father going off on one of his nasty drunken rages or personal attacks. Plus, they had my mother as an amazing example of grace under pressure. No matter what he did or said, it was very clear that my sisters deeply loved and cared about my father and that they would do anything for him.

For a lot of my adult life, this in itself caused an invisible separation between my sisters and me, even long after I moved away from home. Since I couldn't remember experiencing the kinder, gentler Paul W. White, I sometimes found it difficult to relate to my sisters emotionally, and I pulled away and alienated myself. Even though we all had a tough time growing up, my father treated me differently than he treated them. Even if our experiences were similar, they were different because my father and I were both male, and I was always looking to him to be an encouraging example. But his verbal attacks cut me deeply and were impossible to ignore. I felt like I was the only person in the entire household who disliked him.

My sisters took very good care of me, but I didn't have the kind of trust and closeness with any of them that made me feel safe or comfortable enough to confide in them. I was constantly being made to feel like I didn't fit in anywhere. All of this, on top of the humiliating bed-wetting, was emotionally overwhelming.

So, when my sisters would begin to reminisce and tell their "fun stories about Daddy," I would get very quiet or leave the room. I didn't want to rain on the parade, but I didn't want to be the drum major, either. I'd slip away but could still hear my family laughing about difficult situations they'd lived through with him that were now viewed to be somehow humorous. As an adult, I know that laughter is a wonderfully healing medicine and can be a great means of survival and a way of overcoming adversity. But at that time, I could never even imagine finding humor in the experiences I'd had with my father.

Each day I'd come home from school with great trepidation, having no idea what to expect when I opened the door. I never knew what state I'd find my father in.

Our apartment was the second-to-last unit on a cul-de-sac near the end of the complex. When I'd get to the top of our street and start walking toward the house, I would feel the tension and anxiety building. These feelings of panic and fear would increase the closer I got to our door.

My long walk down the street, of course, was frequently accompanied by physical or verbal attacks from the neighborhood bullies, both boys and girls. I was constantly teased and accused of being a sissy who walked and acted like a girl. Furthermore, I was frequently beaten up for the very things that were held up as virtues in the family and at school—things like being polite and respectful, having good manners, and speaking well. We didn't go to church as a family, but we said grace before meals and got down on our knees to say our prayers at bedtime. One of my few pleasant memories of my father is of him teaching me my bedtime prayers.

I never got used to the name-calling, although over time I learned to ignore at least some of it. But they'd always break me when they quoted my own father, who when drunk and belligerent would tell anyone who'd listen how much he wished that he had a son who wasn't such a punk. This would cut straight to my heart as a kid, especially since my father rarely seemed to want anything to do with me.

The closer I'd get to the house, the more I prayed that

my father would still be sober and quiet or that, if he were drunk, he'd be upstairs in his room passed out. When he was sober, no one in the house ever knew how long it would last, and we'd all walk on eggshells as if we could somehow control his appetite for alcohol.

If he were sober, he would most likely be in the living room glued to the only television in the house, watching one of his favorite programs. His few choice words to me were usually something like "*Shhhh* . . . be quiet" or "Change the channel for me." Another was "Run up to the store and get me . . ." These commands were issued from a recliner no one else was allowed to sit in when he was home. Beside it sat his prized foldout dinner tray, which, of course, the rest of us were forbidden to use.

I honestly do not recall my father ever asking me how I was or how school had been that day. Sometimes, I'd put down my books and sit on the couch and try to watch one of his boring programs with him just to spend time with Dad and try and find something in common with him.

My father loved westerns and science fiction. He was a *Star Trek* fanatic and would watch the same episodes over and over! I hated *Star Trek*, but I'd suffer through it for the sake of forging camaraderie. In my limited recollection, my father was not completely sober very often, so I'd seize those opportunities as a chance to see what he was like when he wasn't drunk and belligerent.

Surely, there had to be more to him than the extreme opposites of roaring drunkenness and near-deafening silence.

Fathers and sons on television always got along great. *The Courtship of Eddie's Father*, with Bill Bixby and Brandon Cruz, was one of my favorite shows as a child. I had vivid fantasies of my father and I having great heart-to-heart talks like Eddie and his TV dad. It never occurred to me that there were millions of kids all over the country whose experiences were a lot more like mine than like Eddie's.

The truth is that my father had very little so say when he wasn't drinking. When sober, he seemed timid, shy, and maybe even a little nervous and uncomfortable. The drinking seemed to help him come out of his shell. In the beginning, it would be amazing at first to see the incredible light and personality he was hiding, but before you knew it he was slicing you to shreds. He was like Dr. Jekyll and Mr. Hyde. It was bewildering, and also very sad.

Sometimes during the commercial breaks I'd try to spark a conversation and ask him questions, trying to engage him in discussing what we were watching. This would irritate him and he'd send me outside, the last place I wanted to be since I had so few friends in the neighborhood. Even if I sat there with my father watching television in silence, he would get strangely annoyed and send me away. I was a curious kid, a good student with good grades and tons of questions about life. Yet my father seemed to want nothing to do with me.

On another one of my favorite TV shows, *My Three Sons*, Fred MacMurray's character always praised his sons for their achievements. I couldn't understand why my father didn't seem to be proud of me. I thought that he should be congratulating me for my good grades and good behavior. It felt like he'd rather have had a son who was unruly and bad than one who was intelligent and well mannered. I grew more and more confused and thought that his disliking me was my fault.

I credit the love and nurturing of my mother and sisters for filling in the gaps left empty by my father's distance and verbal attacks. I never doubted my mother's love for me, but it was very apparent that she was overwhelmed. In addition to raising us, she worked full-time at a hotel, and she had an additional part-time job a few days a week assisting a woman on the other side of town. This meant that several times during the week she'd go from one job to the other, traveling by bus. At times, she'd even work at her part-time job on her days off. She'd get home late and tired and then do it all over again. In the middle of all of this, she was somehow miraculously able to cook, supervise, and run the household. Her children all have a committed work ethic and a strong sense of integrity thanks to my mother's unfailing and tireless example.

I walked on eggshells around both of my parents because they appeared to be stressed by their circumstances, and I didn't want to add to it. Sometimes when I had reached my emotional limit with my father's insults, I would go to her in tears and ask her why Daddy disliked me. She would never give me an explanation, try to put words in his mouth, or make excuses for him. She would simply say to me, "Alton, he is still your father." Her saying that would frustrate me to no end because to me it wasn't an answer—and it didn't change anything.

Not understanding alcoholism, never getting a reasonable answer about my father's aggression toward me, and his seemingly being able to get away with any devastation he'd caused left me with the impression that feelings didn't matter.

I AM MY FATHER'S SON

In spite of everything, I could tell by the books he read and how much he loved information that my father was a curious and deeply intelligent man.

It took me many years as an adult to realize that I was a little bit like my father, and when I did, it hit me like a ton of bricks. It occurred to me while watching one of my favorite programs, a documentary series that satisfied my curiosity about how certain things are made and the history of them, what I call "Geek TV." I devour programs on the Discovery Channel, the History Channel, and the National Geographic Channel. And they remind me that, no matter what the history of our relationship,

I am in many crucial ways truly my father's son. These are the exact kinds of programs that most often kept my father glued to the TV all those years.

He also loved reading and would keep stacks of *National Geographic* magazine by his chair. He would read them from beginning to end, and I do the same with books and articles about nature. I definitely get my love of analysis and knowledge from both him and my mother. It took lots of spiritual healing to be able to feel the pride and comfort of these revelations as an adult.

It was a tremendous challenge growing up in a home with a father who suffered from alcoholism, a truly devastating disease. Anyone who grows up in a home with an alcoholic suffers as much if not more than the alcoholic, and it can affect every decision that you make for the rest of your life.

Before writing this book, huge chunks of my childhood memories were missing, which is far from surprising. It has, in fact, been proven that children who suffer trauma, in my case violence resulting from constant bullying, blank out experiences to survive. And it's even more apparent when certain kinds of trauma are repeated continually with seemingly no end in sight. I was one of those children.

I am extremely grateful to the universe that two of the most lifesaving qualities that I discovered about myself as a kid are the gifts of hope and resilience. I was blessed to have eternal optimism, regardless of the circumstances. Challenges beyond my control were constantly threatening my spirit, and I am grateful to God that I was able to maintain an innate enthusiasm for life.

I would escape into my favorite music on the radio, my beloved TV programs, books, and my vivid imagination. I would fantasize and dream about life being better than my present reality.

Enduring negative experiences also helped me develop stamina. I was able to withstand the pressures, move through them, and come out on the other side with the hope and faith that my being different would someday serve me. In fact, my dreams of moving away from the limitations of my neighborhood and the other kids who lived there began as far back as I can remember.

Slowly but surely, I made peace with the fact that I didn't fit in with the other kids or at home, and after a while I stopped trying. I withdrew emotionally and became very quiet, obedient, and shy. I felt that my opinion didn't matter, so I seldom offered it or expressed it. This often led to more victimization, but I held my breath and took it, praying that someday the universe would provide me with the break that I knew in my gut would eventually come.

In an ideal world, children are guaranteed safety and love, and parents stand as a living demonstration of

what the child is striving for and hopes to achieve, both as an individual and as a member of society. The child is to be provided with attention and affection and the things he cannot get for himself until he learns how to meet his own needs. The world, however, is far from ideal, and for many reasons children can find themselves starved for basic necessities, both tangible as well as spiritual and emotional.

Happily, for the adult children of not-as-available parents, we can learn the most important lessons of life from both the positive and negative aspects of parenting. (Even the best parents may have blind spots or shortcomings.) The key is to discover which are which. We hope that the positive aspects are easier to identify. But with awareness and forgiveness, the real jewels of adulthood are found in the process of overcoming childhood challenges. Among those is the overwhelming "unfairness" we feel as children when we don't get what we think or know that we need. But we can learn from our parents' mistakes, as well as our own, how to bypass similar pitfalls. It may take some patience and experience, and the release of some defensive anger or self-pity, but an imperfect childhood is not a lifelong sentence to unhappiness. Fulfillment in life turns out to be a choice.

FOOD FOR THOUGHT

1. In what ways was your childhood nurturing? How was it challenging?

2. How can your life as a child affect self-image, self-esteem, and self-confidence in later life? And how does that affect both your personal and professional life?

3. How can the challenges of an imperfect childhood be turned into advantages later in life?

4. How can our forgiveness of others and ourselves help transform us from fearful children to powerful adults?

Courage doesn't always roar. Sometimes courage is the quiet voice at the end of the day saying, "I will try again tomorrow."

—Mary Anne Radmacher, author

Chapter 4

MICHAEL JACKSON AND THE BUFFER CLOSET

Fantasizing and daydreaming are free and available to all of us. They possess abundant potential as healing tools for coping with situations that may at the time seem insurmountable. But they can do even more than help us escape. They can teach us who we really are. Their resulting inspirations may come in many ways and many forms, and it's vital to be open and accessible to both identify and receive the emotional gifts they can provide.

The linen closet in the bedroom hall was not my only refuge in our crowded home. My other sanctuary was a dark utility closet just off the kitchen at the back of the apartment. It was the only place I had all to myself—well, except for the mops, brooms, household supplies, and my father's equipment for his job cleaning office buildings at night. To me, it was a cozy, safe place where I could let my imagination run wild and be whoever and whatever I wanted to be.

Whether I'd had a tough day at school or in the neighborhood, or difficulty at home, I always knew, no matter what, that I had my own sacred place to go when everyone else in the apartment was preoccupied. I didn't use the words "sacred place" in those days, but that is exactly what it was and how it felt.

So, what was I doing in that small, dark closet, you might ask? I was doing what every little black boy in America my age was doing—pretending to be Michael Jackson!

The Michael Jackson phenomenon was all over television and radio when I was a kid. These were the major sources of information and entertainment in our household, as they were in most. Radio and TV were where I "met" so many of the entertainers who would be important to me.

The people I watched and listened to were the buddies who kept me company after school. It was to them that I escaped when things in my young life felt unbearable. They helped make up for not having close friends I could trust.

I was lucky that variety shows, talk shows, and awards shows with huge production numbers were popular when I was a kid. My family gathered in front of the TV to watch *The Ed Sullivan Show, The Carol Burnett Show, The Sonny & Cher Comedy Hour, Rowan & Martin's Laugh-in,* and the groundbreaking *Flip Wilson Show,* the first network variety series starring an African American. I enjoyed fantasies of someday being one of their "Special Guest Stars." These shows gave me the opportunity to see some of my favorite entertainers sing and dance and then sit down and be interviewed about their lives. It was a total escape for me.

Seeing multitalented performers like Sammy Davis Jr., Harry Belafonte, Johnny Mathis, and all the phenomenal groups from Motown was life altering for a young black boy. My eyes grew wide whenever I'd think about the possibilities abounding beyond the Cincinnati projects.

It's difficult to explain just how powerful it was to see black male entertainers on television not only performing beautifully but appearing well-dressed, well-spoken, and confident. I felt that acquiring the combination of their talents, manners, and education could help me break through the boundaries and limitations of the "projects mentality." Not only did white people seem to expect little of us, but many black people did, too. The men and women I was seeing on television clearly set their goals high—and they were achieving them.

I am grateful to my parents that our family viewing and listening was quite diverse. I grew up listening to Motown and funk, as well as Elton John, Billy Joel, and

Glen Campbell, to name a few. We took in pop, rock, easy listening, country, jazz, and disco. We listened and snapped our fingers to all of it.

To this very day, I can be in a car with a friend and I'll sing along with nearly every song playing on the classic easy listening station. Friends are invariably amazed that I know all the words and melodies to these bygone hits. Many of those very same songs are the ones that I taught myself to harmonize to after seeing them sung and performed on a TV show or hearing them on the radio when I was a boy. I loved all of them. But only one entertainer stood above all—Michael Jackson.

It started when I was around seven or eight and Michael was still just a kid himself. He was the boy wonder, the precocious young leader of the Jackson 5 and, to a fellow black child, a powerful example of what might be possible. I mean, who wouldn't want to be young, famous, rich, and idolized all over the world?

The Jackson brothers were undisputed superstars. They performed at sold-out concerts and enjoyed record-breaking album sales. I was glued to the TV set whenever they made an appearance, with my eyes particularly fixed on Michael, the youngest member of the band at that point and the definite standout with his unmatched charisma and powerful voice. He could sing any style of music, and he had dance moves that every kid I knew imitated, with varying degrees of success. But what really struck me about Michael Jackson was that whenever I saw him on TV he was smiling. He was having a blast. He seemed *happy*, and I wanted some of that for myself.

One of the Jackson 5's biggest hits was "Dancing Machine," which quickly rose to the number one spot on the R & B charts in 1974. I first saw the Jackson 5 perform "Dancing Machine" on *Soul Train*. Michael broke into a dance that became instantly iconic—the robot. The robot involved stiffening your body and isolating your neck and other body parts while pivoting and turning on your feet like a toy robot. I would study every Michael Jackson step, and then I'd take those moves back to the storage closet to rehearse.

Like the linen closet turned bedroom, the utility closet didn't have an actual door. It had a white sheer curtain that allowed just enough of a glow for me to see and not be completely in the dark. In the middle of my refuge sat a huge mechanical contraption called a buffer. This formidable machine was a key component of my father's office-cleaning business. Sometimes, he would actually take me with him to some empty building he had to spiff up. Those rare trips are my favorite childhood memories of him and one of the few times I remember us bonding. I would beg him to let me go with him during the summer when school was out, and once in a while he'd say yes. Usually we'd head out at around eleven at night and not get back until the wee hours of the morning.

The adventure always began with a stop at White Castle for coffee. Their coffee was my father's favorite. He invariably ordered a large "heavy, heavy," which meant heavy sugar and heavy cream. He would order me one too and we'd sit in the car sipping our hot coffees, him preparing for a hard night's work and me preparing for a fun night of pretending. I loved the feeling of us sitting together in the front seat drinking our adult-only beverages. It felt like we were buddies.

My father cleaned all kinds of buildings, and I loved sitting behind the big desks in the enormous chairs having one-way conversations on the phone and telling my invisible secretary to come to my office quickly to take dictation or something equally important. I would often visualize having a desk, an office, and a business of my own, and my father's furnished offices were great real-life sets, with functioning props, where I could practice.

Watching my father clean the floors at the offices was truly fascinating. The buffer was a big, awkward mechanism that took a lot of strength and coordination to maneuver. I would study him using it and, once in a while, he'd let me try. Naturally, I couldn't get the hang of the thing. It was way too heavy for me! You had to hold the machine steady while the bottom of it moved in circles. Every time I'd try, he would have to step in before it went flying across the floor.

Since I was so small, he'd sometimes let me stand on the machine's center platform and ride along while he used it. This was superfun because the machine would vibrate and shake. It would tickle me, and I loved it when I'd let out a sound and my voice would wobble and shake along with it.

Sometimes, my father would let me help him with other things in the buildings, until I'd start to slow him down or get distracted by a cool desk or an office chair that rocked or swiveled. Being up and about at three or four in the morning would start out as a blast, but at some point before dawn, I would peter out and fall asleep somewhere in the building. When it was time to go, my father would scoop me up and carry me to the car. These rare father-and-son nights usually ended with a stop at a twenty-four-hour diner for breakfast before we went back home, having barely spoken all night long.

The silence was peculiar, perhaps, but it was a welcome change from his boozy self or the distant sober version of the man. In fact, I cherished every minute of the calm quiet. During these times, it seemed that he liked me. Letting me go with him and have coffee like a grown-up, carrying me to the car when I feel asleep, and treating me to breakfast made me feel more accepted by him than at any other time. During those few working nights together he didn't say much, but he seemed like a father to me.

When the buffer machine was resting in the utility closet, it was the perfect playmate. It had that large, circular steel base with a round solid platform in the middle that was raised about a foot off the ground, and it had a long handle that ran up the back with handlebars at the top. It looked like a big metal flying saucer with a pogo stick attached. The machine's circular platform was also the perfect stage for a fledgling Michael Jackson impersonator.

In my mind, anything behind the handlebars was my "backstage area." Everything else was reserved for the audience. My microphone? The power cord, of course! And as small as that platform was, I'd still manage to spin and twirl on it, all while switching my microphone/power cord from one hand to the other. The cord was long enough for me to go out into my make-believe audience and single out the prettiest girl to serenade, just like I'd seen Michael do on television.

Even when I wasn't in the utility closet, I daydreamed of scenarios involving the Jackson 5. I would imagine they were going to appear in concert in Cincinnati and that Michael had fallen ill or something, and I was the unknown kid who had to step in to save the show. Or that one of my favorite TV programs, like *The Carol Burnett Show,* was coming to Cincinnati looking for the next young Johnny Mathis, and I would step up to the mike to sing, and everyone would smile and cheer.

In fact, I never sang aloud at my make-believe concerts. I'd only whisper, so that no one else in the apartment could hear me. I never sang in front of anyone. I wished I could have training, but voice or music lessons of any kind were so financially out of the question for my family that I never even bothered to ask.

So, my early "training" was silently mimicking musical numbers I saw on TV or singing along with the radio. I taught myself to harmonize with my favorite artists on the radio or the records my sisters used to play. I am to this very day a huge fan of the 5th Dimension. They were the perfect mix of every kind of music, and their harmonies were so tight that my ears would tingle when I heard them. I would start with the soloist's part and then learn the background harmonies. I spent hours listening closely to discover how they all eventually came together to complete a song. And yet I never sang out loud until I was sure no one else was home.

In fact, I *loved* the sensation of singing and how good it felt in my body. When I sang, my insides would vibrate as if I were being awakened, cleansed, and lightened. The sensations I experienced when singing were soothing, making me feel safe, comfortable, and powerful— all the things I didn't feel when I wasn't singing. Those vibrations tickled me and made me giggle. They made me happy. The more I sang, the better and more hopeful I felt.

My desire to whisper along with the TV or radio and then sneak into the utility closet to perform my sotto voce concerts increased. Looking forward to them became more exciting and frequent, and the daydreaming kept getting more intense. It was so much fun.

As much as I loved the idea of performing in front of a crowd, and as much as I enjoyed how peaceful and at ease singing made me feel, I could never imagine actually having the confidence to share it with anyone, even my family. Painfully shy and supersensitive, I didn't think I could muster the nerve to stand onstage like a real performer. I was afraid that everyone would laugh at me and that I would be embarrassed, shamed, and face even further rejection.

I spent many incredible hours in that closet, rehearsing by myself and performing to thousands of imaginary fans. Although my fantasies in the utility closet were vivid, my fear of what awaited outside it was that much stronger. I knew that in order for my dream to have a chance of becoming a reality, I would have to find the courage to break through my shyness. Or at least that's how *I* remember it. My family has a different version of my baby steps toward show business.

My family tells stories of me as a very small kid singing and dancing in front of the TV. My mother says that I'd watch someone singing and dancing and within minutes would replicate what I saw. They were all amazed at my natural skill and confidence at such a young age. My mother finds it difficult to believe that I do not have the slightest recollection of any of it.

Going back over this odd disparity between my recollection and theirs, I can't really come up with an explanation. Maybe when I was very young I was open with my "performances," and became much more closeted, literally, after my self-esteem plummeted due to the challenges with my father and my classmates. Maybe I associated my talents with the things the school kids would use to bully me. Or maybe, like all traumatized children, I just got so used to blocking things out that I have lost those memories forever. The fact remains, it didn't come as a surprise to my mother or my sisters when I started singing and acting for real.

Among the most important lessons of life is that your dreams and fantasies are personal. They are yours alone. Shyness, shame, self-doubt, and low self-esteem—which are more common than you might expect in the childhoods of amazingly accomplished adults—seem like insurmountable obstacles when we're kids. But they're not. Did you know, for example, that James Earl Jones, the son of an actor, had such a speech impediment as a child that he wouldn't even speak?

Ironically, the very things we naturally love to do often bring us the most uncertainty, the most discomfort. But that's because they are so important to us, and so revealing of who we are. The good news is that the more we let the world see us as we really are, the more support we find from the people who matter. Going forward and doing what we love, whether it's singing or sports or making robots, can actually give us the will and the nerve to pursue our dreams. And developing and maintaining the courage to continue investing in them can put us on course to realizing our wildest fantasies of success and making them come true.

FOOD FOR THOUGHT

1. What are your earliest childhood memories of what you wanted to do when you grew up?

2. How did your happiest childhood memories make you feel? And does your personal and professional life make you feel like that?

3. What did you do to claim your own identity as a child, even when your solution was imperfect or a kind of compromise?

4. How is compromising a pitfall? How is it a survival technique? How does it help you achieve your goals?

5. Can you see the long-term benefits of optimism and positive thinking even when life situations seem grim or difficult? How can optimism get us through to the next step?

When you recover or discover something that nourishes your soul and brings joy, care enough about yourself to make room for it in your life.

—Jean Shinoda Bolen, psychiatrist

Chapter 5

EDUCATING ALTON

Education and a willingness to learn can transform insecurity and lack of self-esteem into decisiveness and self-assurance and become tools for establishing and maintaining confidence. Whatever you learn and acquire mentally can never be taken from you unless you allow it.

I attended Frederick Douglass Elementary. The school still exists in the same place in Cincinnati on Park Avenue, but it has been modernized. I loved school and was one of those kids who was so excited about the first day back each September that I could barely sleep the night before. There was something wonderful to me about the newness of it, the potential: a new grade, a new teacher, and new possibilities. And I couldn't wait to show off my brand-new school clothes!

In some ways being at school felt more comfortable than home. I loved that school provided predictability and required discipline. The icing on the cake for me was being rewarded with good grades and receiving approval for doing good work.

At Frederick Douglass, it was a huge honor when a teacher would ask a student to stay after class to help them with extra assignments like organizing or grading papers. It was an indication that the teacher liked you, trusted you, and thought you were responsible enough to handle the task. *Nothing* pleased me more than being the prized student who was picked. I loved staying after school to help, particularly because it delayed my having to go home and deal with my neighborhood challenges.

I was a naturally gifted kid, but my shyness often held me back. I would often know the correct answer to the problem on the board, but I was too self-conscious to raise my hand. I was afraid that the kids would give me a hard time or accuse me of trying to show off. I didn't like drawing attention to myself, and yet I longed for approval and recognition at the same time. I am so grateful that my teachers challenged me and didn't let me hide in the back of the room with the other kids whose last names were near the end of the alphabet. Even though I didn't raise my hand, teachers called on me and asked me to answer difficult math and spelling questions.

Being forced to speak up and having the right answer gave me much-needed validation. The more often my teachers called on me, the more comfortable and confident I became about raising my hand to participate. Their belief in me helped minimize the embarrassment and self-consciousness I felt in front of my classmates.

Teachers favored me because I was quiet, respectful, and attentive. Except, of course, when I was fantasizing, daydreaming, or doodling during class, which I was inclined to do. I liked drifting off and drawing shapes and patterns and letting my fantasies run wild. My imagination was really the only wild thing about me.

Besides math, my favorite class was art. I was afraid to sing in front of anyone, but art class was a place I could express myself without having to say a word. When I was in the fourth grade, my art teacher took notice of a collage I made with shapes that I'd drawn, cut out, and glued to a piece of construction paper. She marveled at my creation and told me that I had talent. She said that she'd like to speak with my parents about sending me to a new arts school named the School for Creative and Performing Arts, which had just opened in the city. I had immediate fantasies of finally getting away from the rough kids I was stuck dealing with to attend a school in another neighborhood with a new set of kids who were creative and artistic.

I floated on a cloud of anticipation the whole week leading up to the meeting I had with my art teacher and my mother. My teacher explained that this new school was designed for gifted, intelligent kids, which made me even more thrilled about going there. Unfortunately, my excitement was cut short.

Because the school was so new and my mother felt that she didn't have enough information, she said no. I pleaded with her to at least let me interview for the school, but she wouldn't budge. She explained to me that her chief concerns were my grades and that she did not want me to be distracted. My mother knew that I was being bullied, but many years passed before I told her the extent to which I was already exceedingly distracted at Douglass. Everyone in my family, including my parents, had gone to Douglass. My window of opportunity to break away from that tradition slammed shut, and there was absolutely nothing that I could do about it. I was heartbroken to have lost the great opportunity to go to another school, especially an artistic one.

Given no other choice, I eventually got over the great disappointment and put more energy into being an even better student, hoping to be prepared for any future opportunities.

At that young age, I was hungry for guidance and positive goals. Being a good student made me feel important, accomplished, powerful, and self-reliant. The approval of my teachers made me feel accepted in ways that none of the teasing and name-calling from the other kids could diminish. For me, this was the key to building the endurance I needed to withstand the bullying at school, at home, and in the projects. It gave me hope that I might have a bright future beyond my present reality. I couldn't see it, but I could sense it.

My parents constantly stressed the importance of having a good education and emphasized that it was something that could never be taken away from me. I am blessed that education was so important to my parents and that school was not a burden that I dreaded.

Being a good kid was challenging not only because I felt like a misfit, but also because, like everyone else, I wanted friends and I wanted to belong. I wasn't an *over*achiever, but I was achieving to the full extent of what was clearly an above-average level. I was far more interested in impressing my teachers than causing disturbances and getting into trouble, and this did not make me popular. I was a nerd, plain and simple, and being the "teacher's pet" made it even harder to gain acceptance from the other kids.

However . . . for a good kid and a good student, I had a surprisingly large number of fights after school, mostly for reasons that I did not understand. There were instances where a kid would call me out to fight after school just because I got the best grade on a test or some other assignment. So, there I was after school surrounded by a crowd of rowdy kids, defending myself because some classmate who probably hadn't even studied was bothered that I had done well. I *hated* fighting, but after years of getting beaten up, I could no longer just stand there getting hit for no reason. I detested the confrontations, but I eventually accepted that defending myself against the bullies was a regular part of my school experience.

Despite it all, I did have some school friends. Two of my closest were Robert Tingle and Harvey Benford, and they were very competitive classmates. The three of us had fun vying with each other for the best grades. I would sometimes go to their homes to visit or study after school, but they never came to mine. I met members of their families, but they rarely asked about mine. It didn't bother me because I never felt comfortable bringing friends home to visit. I envied the fact that they had family and friends to help them study.

Everyone at my house seemed so engrossed in his or her own life, so I studied and relied on myself. I never *blamed* my family, and it honestly didn't bother me. We were all doing the best we could under the circumstances. My siblings were loving and supportive, just a bit preoccupied. I was grateful that I had a curiosity and natural affinity for learning that propelled me forward and enabled me to focus.

My two buddies knew little of my home life, but they definitely knew that I was constantly belittled. Neither of them judged me and they would often come to my defense at school. I felt proud that they acknowledged that I was sharp enough to compete with them academically and that they respected me as a peer. Our teachers took note of our rivalry, and one of the three of us was almost always chosen to read aloud in class.

One time I won the competition of the moment but still felt like the loser. It involved our yearly music program. I was already deep in my daydreams and utility-closet fantasies, and I wanted the chance to finally be a part of something similar to what I'd seen on TV. Unfortunately, because I was the best reader, I was picked to be the narrator. I was devastated, because I really wanted to be in the show. The kids who were cast got lines to study and songs to sing. The performers got to be center stage, but as the narrator, I just stood on the side of the stage at a microphone and read. My feelings were hurt because my role didn't seem as important as those of the lead performers—or as much fun.

Harvey and Robert were cast in the play, but they didn't even want to be. They had both wanted to be the narrator, so to them, I had won. They thought I would be happy, but instead I was disappointed and glum. My teacher, Mrs. Dula, tried to convince me that it was an honor to be chosen as the narrator in the show because I spoke so well. But nothing she could say made me feel any less isolated and left out. (At least I was beginning to understand what was really important and exciting to me.)

The performance was in the school's big auditorium, and at showtime I smiled, did my best, and read the assigned narration. After the show, many of the parents and teachers patted me on the back and congratulated me for having such a strong speaking voice and fine diction. I was flattered but found it a bit confusing. I didn't quite know how to take it. The adults complimented me for the same abilities that a lot of their children were constantly teasing and tormenting me about. In order to be "cool," I even tried swearing and talking tough like some of the bad kids, but it didn't suit me, and I still got harassed for sounding too "proper." I couldn't win for losing.

Black History Week

Back in my days at Frederick Douglass Elementary, there was no Black History Month. At least at our school, though, there was a Black History *Week* in February, and a huge deal was made of it, as you would expect from a school named after the most important black abolitionist in American history. I looked forward to it every year. As a black male kid who always found inspiration in positive role models, I looked forward to the big celebratory Black History programs held in the school auditorium. It was a powerful opportunity to recognize the brave people who looked like me and had overcome such unbelievable obstacles. I was confident that if they could do what they did back then, then I could conceivably go even further because of their examples of strength, faith, and determination.

The speeches about our namesake, Frederick Douglass, along with those focusing on Harriet Tubman, Booker T. Washington, and Sojourner Truth, to name a few, reinforced my consciousness and pride for my ancestors' resilience and our ability to survive as a people. The fact that people who were once bound by the horrors of slavery were able not only to overcome their experience but also to excel and accomplish things that made it into history books just amazed me.

It was disappointing to me that so little was expected of me as a black male child and future black man. To my young eyes, black men's free hard labor had made an enormous contribution to the growth and prosperity of the country. For many black male children, it is innately understood that the world can be a very difficult place. Growing up in public housing, I sensed that things would be much harder to accomplish for me and my friends than for other men, white men.

I understood that getting positive acknowledgment as black men takes much more effort, often to the point of overcompensation, just to be considered valid by society. In my young eyes, most black men seemed strong, buoyant, and nurturing—in a tough-love kind of way. Many of the black men I observed, even my father, were somehow able to express their irritations with the limitations imposed on them by society with a reasonably well-adjusted combination of frustration and infectious humor.

During Black History Week, contemporary black heroes were also acknowledged. Powerful men like the Reverend Martin Luther King Jr., actors Sidney Poitier and Harry Belafonte, social activists like Julian Bond and Andrew

Young, and John H. Johnson, founder of Johnson Publishing Company, were living heroes with great ambitions and accomplishments to match. They were incredible examples that, despite an especially difficult road, hard work, dedication, and focus could lead to success and respect.

These black men were exceptional, and I wanted to be like them. I believed that if they could make their dreams come true, then the world could possibly be my oyster too—if I worked hard enough.

To this day, I am grateful that I had the resilience, motivation, hunger, and thirst to be inspired by the examples of past and present role models. Thankfully, I had angels in the form of nurturing adults and educators who embraced me and assured me that it was great that I wanted to be a bright, well-behaved, and well-spoken young man.

It was difficult for me to see the importance of these virtues, these assets, because they came naturally to me. It wasn't a huge struggle for me to be respectful, study hard, or speak well. It is my particular good fortune, for which I am grateful, that I was encouraged by the people who mattered. My family and teachers assured me that my discipline and nascent integrity would pay off if I fed them and kept them in my heart.

As it happened, our neighborhood actually had a place in the history we were learning in school. The projects were only a few blocks away from a beautiful house on Gilbert Avenue that stuck out as something different and significant. I passed that house every day on my way to school, and each time I walked by, I felt a wonderful energy and I sensed that it was someplace special. Eventually I found out that it was the Harriet Beecher Stowe House, home of the abolitionist author of *Uncle Tom's Cabin*, the phenomenally important 1852 novel that brought to light the horrors of slavery in a form that anyone who could read could understand. When I discovered the historical significance of the house, I realized why I had always been so spiritually drawn to it.

Cincinnati sits directly across the Ohio River from Kentucky. The infamous Mason-Dixon Line includes the Ohio River as part of its division between the North, including Ohio, and the slave states in the South. Crossing the bridge over the Ohio River into the city of Cincinnati was a life-changing milestone to slaves who had escaped the South. Cincinnati was freedom. I strongly believe that the slaves who survived the dangerous and treacherous expedition from the South to Cincinnati planted the seeds for me to begin the wonderful life that I am living today.

GOING TO CHURCH

In the summertime, when a lot of the kids in my neighborhood went down south to visit their relatives, I was one of the few kids on my block left behind. We were the only family in the projects that I knew of that didn't have close ties to our relatives in the South. I'd ask my mother why we never ventured down there to visit any of our folks, and she would tell me that no one on either side of our family was in touch with those relatives. I always found this strange. Surely we had to have Southern kinfolk. Why was there no communication with them?

Missing out on those kinds of trips and having no known family ties to the South meant that I had the extremely rare experience of growing up as a black person with an exclusively Northern, urban experience. A lot of the kids would come back in July or August with great stories about huge meals consisting of food grown on their families' farms, of getting up early to get fresh eggs from the chicken coop for breakfast, and of walking for miles on red dirt roads. It sounded like so much fun to travel with your family to visit relatives in another part of the country. Frankly, I was envious—because if the school year was a trial, summer was a lonely bore.

Since I was stuck at home, I was signed up for Vacation Bible School every year up to the sixth grade. Bible school was held at Zion Hope Missionary Baptist Church, which still exists. It is a big, beautiful church across the street from the projects. I loved Vacation Bible School. I was fascinated by the magical stories and wonderful potential for transformation that we'd read about in class. I was also surrounded by teachers, which always made me feel safe. During the school year, I took Bible study as a class once a week. The classes were held across the street from Douglass at Brown Chapel A.M.E. (African Methodist Episcopal), so continuing my studies every summer at Zion Hope felt natural.

In fact, I wasn't raised in a strict religious environment, but I am very thankful to my parents that prayer, gratitude, and the acknowledgment of a higher being were enforced in our household. Although we never attended church regularly as a family, I felt drawn to church at a very young age. And one of my earliest and richest memories, from when I was about five or six years old, is tied to a church.

Zion Hope Missionary Baptist was next to the big neighborhood playground one street over from where I lived on Mathers Street. While I played in the sand and swung on the swings, I watched the people coming in and out of the church. The adults and children going in were well-dressed and looked pleasant and happy, and they'd come out smiling, singing, and looking even happier than when they'd entered. I was curious about what was going on in there that made people so joyful and kept them coming back.

For weeks and weeks, I begged one sister after another to take me to a service at that church, and every time they would promise to take me the next week. Sunday would come and I'd wake them, but they'd give me some kind of an excuse, put it off until the next Sunday, and then go back to sleep. On one of those Sunday mornings, tired of being put off, I asked if I could just go by myself. Half-asleep, one of my sisters said yes. Nervous but excited, I ran to the closet to find my best outfit. I picked out some pants, a shirt, a jacket, and a clip-on tie and darted out the door to the church. All I knew was that this was the day that I was finally going to find out what was happening inside of the magical building.

I sensed that I was going to be let in on a huge secret. I walked into the church vestibule and was greeted at the front door by some very well-dressed kids around my age. They must have been child ushers or some such thing. Then a woman approached me and asked me if I was looking or waiting for someone. I told her no and asked if it was okay for me to go inside and sit down. She looked at me oddly, clearly puzzled that I didn't have an adult with me, but hesitantly said yes.

I pulled open the tall doors and stepped into the sanctuary of the church. I was struck by how big and tall everything seemed. The congregation was standing and singing and rocking from side to side, clapping their hands. I remember being mesmerized by the beauty of the stained glass windows. When the song ended, I walked down the long middle aisle, said "Excuse me" to two adults on the end, and sat in the middle of a pew on the left side of the church. I do not remember what was said or sung, but I do remember how wonderful I felt that Sunday morning in that sanctuary.

By the time I floated back home after the service, my sisters were awake and worried. They had been looking all over for me. I told them what I had done, and they were shocked and upset. They asked me not to tell Mama when she got home from work. They said that if she found out that I had gone a whole street over from where we lived all by myself at that age—while they were all still asleep in bed—we would all get into big trouble.

Well, Mama did find out, as mamas all over the world invariably do. On her way home from work later that evening, she ran into one of my sisters' friends who had seen me at church that morning. She told my mother that she was happy to see me but that she was surprised I was there by myself and dressed in mismatched clothes that didn't fit. I don't remember the punishment, but experiencing the beautiful peace that I felt in church that morning made it well worth it.

After that Sunday morning, I found myself looking for any and every sign of a religious or higher power. I was open and felt naturally drawn to anything having to do with growth and transformation, even though I didn't have words to describe it at the time. It was a purely instinctive feeling. Oddly—or perhaps not so oddly, given my future as an actor—I found all those things in two of my favorite movies: *The Wizard of Oz* and *The Ten Commandments*.

I couldn't wait until they came on television every year. Their messages were insightful and transported me to other places, giving me hope for better times ahead. Even as a kid I comprehended that in *The Wizard of Oz*, Dorothy's real journey beyond all the flying monkeys, sleep-inducing poppy fields, and the Emerald City was really about finding herself, and that all of the characters represented powerful aspects that were already inside her.

The Ten Commandments fascinated me because it demonstrated that there was something greater than myself that could lead me to another kind of life. Moses's journey showed me that magic could happen in my life, that the adult life ahead of me could be better than my present circumstances if I believed in a powerful energy that I couldn't see but that I could sense.

This was the beginning of my budding spirituality and the long slow building of my personal faith. It fostered an increasing awareness that I had an invisible friend who understood and accepted me, an ideal friend who would also guide and protect me—a loving, present brother and accepting father that I had been waiting for, and seeking to find.

＊＊＊＊＊＊

My understanding of spirituality is establishing a relationship not only with an entity called God, but with the universe as a whole. For me, spirituality is not limited to a specific religion. Developing and nurturing an intimate relationship with a higher source, however you define it, helps maintain faith, optimism, and endurance.

The world we live in offers many kinds of religious and spiritual experiences, and they are sometimes at odds with one another. Some religious people think that personal programs of spiritual education and enlightenment are not legitimate, but that a person must participate in a particular, organized faith. Some individuals who practice a wide variety of personal disciplines descended from ancient practices on every continent of our globe believe that organized religion actually prevents enlightenment, or at least that it is unnecessary. And some of these people are extremely passionate in their beliefs.

My experience is that there is no need to choose one or the other. A person can practice meditation and still attend church on Sunday, or worship at a synagogue or mosque. The choices are endless and personal. What matters is what resonates with you, what speaks to your heart, or, if you will, your soul. Judging others for making different choices is, I think, a mistake.

I am clear in my own mind that a spiritual approach to life, some sort of awareness of a greater being, has been necessary to my own development and my own success—both when things were not going the way I might have liked and when they were. But I hesitate to say that you cannot achieve success without some kind of inner, spiritual life. My experience is that life would be a lot less meaningful, and sometimes harder to endure, without it. And I have a sneaking suspicion that a great many people who succeed in living out their greatest dreams share an involvement in some kind of religious or spiritual path. It is, of course, entirely up to you.

FOOD FOR THOUGHT

1. What was your school experience like? How do you think it helped shape you? How much of it was positive? How much did you have to redefine later in life in order to move on?

2. Teasing and bullying can be devastating to a child, but can they help you develop an inner strength that might be valuable for your adult life?

3. How can we learn from the disappointments of our childhoods and not carry defeatist feelings into our adult lives?

4. How can finding out something about yourself make you feel proud and help you overcome any outside messages that tell you that you are not worthy or valuable enough?

5. Can you ever remember a time or incident when you "took the bull by the horns" to get something you *knew* you needed or wanted?

6. What was the role of religion or spirituality in your childhood, and what is it now? How does it affect the choices you make in your personal and professional lives?

I certainly believe that being in contact with one's spirit and nurturing one's spirit is as important as nurturing one's body and mind. We are three-dimensional beings: body, mind, spirit.

—Laurence Fishburne, actor

Chapter 6

WE THE PEOPLES

Your instincts are a unique gift to help guide you throughout your life, and they belong to you entirely. Learning to trust your gut feeling can provide the courage needed to face opposition or go against the grain, if necessary. Learning to trust your instincts takes time, but when you get there, your instincts will help ensure that you are moving in the right direction.

After finishing Frederick Douglass Elementary, everyone in my family went on to Sawyer Junior High and then Withrow High School. I dreaded having to follow in their footsteps because it would mean staying with the same group of kids. I was desperate for the chance to break away.

My big opportunity came in the sixth grade when I tested well enough to be selected for a junior high school (what we now call middle school) with a great college prep program. It was called Walter Peoples Junior High. I'd never heard of it, but I was excited about getting away and being in a new environment. Peoples turned out to be located in Hyde Park, an upper-class white community in Cincinnati that was the exact opposite of the projects and miles away from where I lived.

Near the end of sixth grade, I was given paperwork to take home to my mother with instructions for her to fill it all out so that my school records could be transferred. I reminded my mother over and over, but the next thing I knew, the school year had come to an end and the paperwork still hadn't been filled out for me to turn in. My mother promised me that she would take care of it by the beginning of the next school year. All through the summer I nagged her about mailing in the papers, and she kept saying she'd get to it.

The feeling of freedom I had that summer made it one of the best I'd ever had in the projects, because I knew that this would be the first time since preschool that I would finally be going away, to a school with students I didn't know. The morning of what was supposed to be my first day at the glorious new school arrived, and I still had no idea where it was or how to get there. After bathing and getting dressed, I approached my mother about what to do, and she confessed that she had never gotten around to sending in the paperwork. She said that she was sorry and that I would have to go to Sawyer Junior High like everyone else.

It's hard to describe the devastation that I felt. My chance to break away was as simple as her filling out a few papers, and she had let me down. I felt a rush of anger come over me unlike anything I'd ever felt before. I told her that if I could not go to Peoples, I was not going to school at all. It was the first time that I ever stood up to my mother.

She looked at me like I was crazy, and I stood there looking at her defiantly. My look alone told her I expected her to do something to correct this. She was stunned because she'd never seen me this way before. For me, continuing to deal with the attacks I'd been tolerating since I'd first started going to school was absolutely not an option.

My mother found the form and called the school. She was told that they had my name and nothing else. After she hung up the phone, she told me that she didn't know what to do. The only advice that she could offer was for me to go to the school in Hyde Park and find out what I could. I was basically on my own. It just so happened that one other person in the projects, a girl named Yvette, had been admitted to the school as well. We had spent a lot of time that summer fantasizing about how exciting it would be to go to a school that was so foreign to us. I ran out of the house and up the street, hoping to catch her before she left to see how she was getting to this new school. Just as I was approaching her door, she and her sister walked out of their apartment.

Yvette told me that her older sister was riding the bus with her to Hyde Park to make sure that she got to Peoples safely on the first day. I asked if I could tag along and they said sure. This was my first time ever taking a bus to school. I had been mailed a bus pass over the summer for transportation and was relieved that I wouldn't have to make this first trip to a new school in a new community all by myself. The timing felt like divine order, although I wouldn't have called it that then.

When I arrived at the school, I went to the main office and gave a woman behind the desk my name. I told her what happened with my mother and she confirmed that they had my name and that I had been accepted to the school, but nothing else. I started to panic, but then I asked the only question that I could think of: "May I please go here?" She said of course I could.

I breathed a huge sigh of relief, because if she had turned me away, I don't know what I would have done or where I would have gone that day. She gave me my homeroom assignment based on my last name, told me that I would have to sort of "wing it" for the first few days, and said that once they got my transcripts from Douglass Elementary, I would get a regular schedule.

It was so liberating to know that I was going to have new opportunities to reinvent myself; but, conversely, it was devastating to me that my mother had not come through for me. I knew that she hadn't done it on purpose, but it hurt me deeply to have almost missed this incredible opportunity. But I knew how hard my mother worked and that she was often overwhelmed juggling everything, and I knew in my heart she was doing the best that she could.

So, instead of holding a grudge, which would have only hurt me more, I focused on the gratitude for what was about to be a new life ahead, one that I could define and orchestrate myself. The excitement of the new possibilities that awaited far outweighed any residual hurt tied to my mother's forgetfulness.

Walter Peoples was the first time that I would experience going to school with white kids. I was neither bothered nor intimidated. It was a racially mixed school, and most of the students were intelligent and mature. At Peoples, I was almost immediately accepted for the very same things that I had been teased about most of my life. I garnered positive reinforcement for my intellect, for speaking well, and for being a gentleman.

And while at Peoples, I also got a lot of attention for my fashion sense, and I became somewhat of a trendsetter. It was at Peoples that I finally had the opportunity to express myself through my appearance. I had discovered *GQ* and *Ebony* magazines, and I'd flip through the pages and fantasize about being one of the handsome, stylish models with fashionable clothes.

Back-to-school clothing at the beginning of the school year and an Easter Sunday outfit were the extent of the new clothes that my mother was able to afford unless something became too worn out to wear any longer. I was never given a regular allowance as a kid, because we couldn't afford it. If I really wanted something outside of my basic needs, I would have to find a way to pay for it myself—and I did. In the summers, I would babysit my sisters' kids and work part-time at a shoe factory warehouse to make money.

I learned to be practical. I learned the value of money and the importance of saving. When I started working, I contributed a certain amount to my mother and I saved the rest for the things that I wanted, which allowed me to experiment with clothing and find my own style. My father wasn't available to teach me about adolescence and my growing maturity, so I had to figure out what manhood meant to me and define it on my own. I used my imagination and my money to model my appearance after the confident-looking men I saw on the pages of *GQ* and *Ebony*. At first I was self-conscious about expressing my style, but the compliments from students and teachers helped my confidence.

Peoples is where one of the many dichotomies in my life became apparent for the first time as well. While I thrived at Peoples both socially and academically, I had to return home to the same neighbors and same mindset that pervaded the projects. Fortunately, the long walks down the long street to my apartment became less painful. Now, the boys who had teased me all those years had nothing to say. It was clear that all the kids in my neighborhood who had gone on to Sawyer had basically stayed the same. I had moved on.

I will never forget the last time that I walked down that street and one of the guys said something threatening to me. I stopped and just looked at him. He stared back at me, waiting for the usual look of fear or hurt on my face, but there was none. I knew and he knew—as did his gang of boys—that the balance of power had shifted. Their opinion of me meant nothing. While they were stuck in the past, I had already moved toward a bright future. For the first time in any of our lives, these same boys started greeting me and saying hello, which slowly evolved into their asking me about my new school and, miraculously, to their encouraging me to do well there.

It's amazing to think of all the years I spent trying to gain the acceptance and approval of the bullies in my neighborhood. Now I was I finally getting it, but I no longer needed it. The more I healed, the more I actually began to feel sorry for them. I began to wonder if they had treated me badly because someone had been victimizing them. How else would they have learned or known to do it? I also became aware of how blessed I was to be able to get out, to break the cycle and discover a life outside of our neighborhood.

By this point, all my sisters had moved out, and I was the only child at home with my parents. My mother still worked harder than I wished she had to, and my father still drank, and occasionally they'd fight. It was difficult being the only child with them at times, especially when things got heated, but I balanced it with my new life and new social activities at school.

For the first time, there were kids in my life I considered friends, both black and white, many of whose families were middle or upper-middle class. They'd invite me over to their houses after school to study or to have dinner. It was especially eye-opening to witness how some of my middle-class black friends lived.

But as much as I enjoyed hanging out with them at their homes after school, one thing about my life didn't change. I knew that I would never be able to reciprocate and take them home with me. Whenever they'd ask to come to my house, I'd make up an excuse about its being too far away or something. I had even greater shame of where I lived after seeing their big, beautifully decorated homes. Even the thought of bringing one of my friends to the projects and walking in the door to find my father drunk was mortifying, so I never let it happen.

My life outside of Peoples was a complete mystery to all my classmates. I didn't lie to them; I just never gave them any details. None of my friends at school knew anything about my parents or what they did for a living. I didn't care that they didn't know. The most important thing to me was building a new life in a new, nurturing environment and learning as much as I could.

It was thrilling and strange for me to be living in two different worlds. At school, I was living a fantasy life, like the ones I saw on TV. I went from being the odd kid who didn't belong, to being at a new school where I fit in perfectly. By the end of my first year at Peoples, I was voted on to the student council and student government. I was also given a special honor, the magnitude of which I only realized later in life.

Peoples Junior High was interviewing for a new principal for the following year, and a group was assembled for the review process: two teachers, two parents, and two students. I was one of the two students selected to be a part of the interviewing panel. I actually have a certificate from the Cincinnati Board of Education commending me for my service. Needless to say, given where I came from, this kind of validation was nothing short of thrilling.

MY EARLY SOLO CAREER: STEPPING OUT OF THE CROWD

My life at church added another dimension that was a secret to my family and my school friends. Brown Chapel A.M.E. was where I had been going to Bible study since elementary school. By this point, I had begun attending services there on my own. After volunteering to be an usher at the church and observing the gospel choir, I finally worked up enough nerve to sign up. Not having to audition made it easy. I could just show up, sing along with everyone else at rehearsals, and enjoy the music.

I loved school, but I also loved singing, even though most of my singing was still being done only in private. I was soon informed, however, that one of the rules of the choir was that everyone eventually had to do a solo. This frightened me, though I reasoned the choir was of a good size, so it would take a while to get around to me. In time, my number came up and I politely passed. The thought of singing solo in front of anyone was still paralyzing.

After the next cycle of solos came and went, I tried to pass again, but the musical director wouldn't accept it. She said that I'd been in the choir for more than a year and that I had to do it. I did my best to wiggle out of it and made every excuse that I could think of, but she held firm. She promised that she'd give me the easiest song there was, with a repeating chorus.

When most people were assigned their solos, they were thrilled and couldn't wait to rehearse and perform them. I did not share that feeling. I was terrified. I panicked as soon as I got to rehearsal, because I was consumed by the pressure to find the courage to make it happen.

At first I sang the solo softly under my breath and was barely audible. Then the musical director sang the song along with me before I finally worked up enough nerve to sing it aloud by myself. I could sense that the choir was becoming irritated and impatient with my excuses, which pushed me to finally stand up and do it. When I finished singing, the choir was encouraging, told me that I sounded pretty good, and that I'd be fine. I didn't really believe them, but their encouragement was reassuring. It felt good to release the tension and finally get through it. This entire process had taken me months, and now the ultimate challenge was to perform it in front of the congregation.

The dreaded Sunday morning came and the musical director nodded for me to go up to the microphone. I stood there trembling as the intro to the song played. Where was the confidence that I had doing my full-out concerts in the closet? What was stopping me from tapping into that? I wondered to myself. I didn't know where to look, so I looked up at the ceiling. When the time came to sing, I did so as strongly as I could. After my solo, there was applause and some "Amens" from the congregation. I went back to my seat light-headed, relieved, and proud that I'd actually gotten through it without passing out or worse.

After the service, a woman in the congregation approached me excitedly, smiling with a look of astonishment on her face. She reached out her hands and pulled me into a hug. She grabbed my face and, looking straight into my eyes, began raving about the power and quality of my voice. She told me that I had something special and that she was very proud of me. I will never forget her kind words or the look on her face that Sunday morning.

Peoples Junior High was a college prep school, but there were also obligatory music classes. Every year there was a spring and a winter concert. For the choir, there were only a couple of guest solo and duet spots. But one of them was the showstopper "Be a Lion" from *The Wiz*. By my second year at Peoples, the boy who had sung the part of the Lion had left for high school, and the music teacher needed a new male voice for the slot. I wanted to do it, but again I was scared. This time there was more at stake because I was among my new peers. Old fears of not fitting in and being teased came back.

My new friends accepted me, but what if I couldn't deliver and their opinion of me changed? Would I be teased again? Would the shame and fear of not being accepted put me in jeopardy in my new environment if I made a fool out of myself in front of the whole class? After taking my teacher and fellow school choir members through a similar exercise in self-consciousness and fear, similar to what I had done with my church choir earlier, I wound up auditioning and getting the spot. Of course, it helped that none of the other boys wanted to do it.

The night of the performance came and the "Be a Lion" duet was a smash! I had never experienced a feeling as wonderful as the wave of applause that came after I sang that evening. I had never done anything that was so easy and received so much praise for it. The next school day, my teachers and fellow classmates seemed awestruck after seeing and hearing me sing onstage, and it added to my growing popularity. I was thrilled with the compliments but even happier that I had come closer to tapping into the energy and fun that I'd experienced doing my private concerts in the closet.

It was then that I was able to recognize that I'd been given something special. It had been difficult to work up to it, but once I got there, it was relatively easy to do. It occurred to me that if I could find a way to let it flow out of me, I could touch more people with my singing. It seemed to make people so happy.

In my final year at Peoples, before going off to high school, I was given solos for both the winter and spring festivals. My music teacher, Mrs. Turner, encouraged me to audition for the Cincinnati School for Creative and Performing Arts, the same one that my mother had forbidden me to interview for back in the third grade. I was equal parts thrilled and terrified at the prospect of going to that amazing school. Being accepted there would be such a dream come true that it became psychologically overwhelming. As wonderful as it might have been, I just could not fathom it actually happening.

I sometimes stayed after school to help Mrs. Turner with extra class work, just as I'd done for my favorite teachers at Douglass Elementary, and she talked to me about the performing arts school. Instead of following my instinct and letting Mrs. Turner set up the audition, I kept hearing the practical voice of my mother in my head saying, *Stay on your academic path*. Admittedly, I also used my mother's voice as an excuse to hide behind my fear of being rejected from something I wanted so badly.

After my very last day at Peoples Junior High, I left the building and headed home. As I was getting on the bus, the finality of the ending of this magical chapter of my life hit me like a ton of bricks, along with the brutal reality that I would now be going to Withrow High School and rejoining all the kids in my neighborhood at school. Completely in a state of panic, I got off the bus and ran back to Mrs. Turner's office, praying that she'd still be there. Thankfully she was. I begged her to call Performing Arts to see if it wasn't too late for me to audition.

Needless to say, she was very upset with me. Because just as I had badgered my mother about turning in the forms for me to go to Peoples, Mrs. Turner had done the same with me about auditioning for Performing Arts—and this time I was the one who had blown it! I had let my fear of jumping into yet another new world become more powerful than the desire to take a chance to more fully develop as a creative person. Mrs. Turner promised that she would do the best that she could and asked for my home phone number to update my parents. (I have since learned that before we can really learn the lessons of our own life's dramas, the scenarios often must repeat themselves with a shift in the cast of characters.)

When I did get back on the bus again to head home that last day at Peoples, all I could think about was having had this wonderful life-changing experience for the past three years and now going backward to the same realities that I'd already escaped once. It was by divine order that I had to pass Withrow High School every day on my bus ride to and from Peoples. As I passed it on that final day, I got depressed and fearful that all my hard-earned growth could be blocked or even undone if my next stop were this school. I could not grasp even the idea of going to Withrow. I had come too far in the past three years, and whether I liked it or not, there was no turning back.

Early the next day, my mother got a call from Mrs. Turner informing us that she had arranged an audition for later that morning. My mother had recently gotten her driver's license and bought herself a brand-new car. She had grown tired of taking the bus and depending on others for transportation. With hard work and focus, she actually purchased a car before she even had her temporary license, though I think the vehicle helped her stay determined to pass the test and make it happen. My mother's many examples of strength and triumph continue to inspire me.

When I asked my mother if she would come with me to the audition, she offered to drop me off at the school and told me that if I wanted it, that it was up to me to make it happen. Unlike my last transfer from one school to the next, I was now fine being on my own and actually rather preferred it. As she drove me down to the school, she reiterated that no matter how things turned out, I had to keep my grades up. She kissed me and wished me luck.

I found my way to the main office and checked in. I had expected to be nervous about auditioning, but my excitement outweighed my fear even though I knew that there was a lot at stake. That morning, I met with different teachers and auditioned for every department—except band, because I didn't play an instrument. Before I left the School for Creative and Performing Arts that afternoon, I was informed that I had been accepted into the school as a vocal music major with a drama minor. My life was about to change again, and I could not have been more excited!

The better the relationship you have with yourself and what it is that you ultimately desire, the clearer the path will be. It will also be easier to summon the courage to trust what is right for you on your journey at any given moment. But these are not lessons that are learned overnight. You can take a lifetime to understand them, and even then, you might need to remind yourself con-

stantly about your essential value to the world. Always remember: be who you are, because everyone else is taken!

Being afraid to stand out in a crowd generally comes from our failure or refusal to acknowledge our own value. Heaven knows it's easy to internalize the things people say to and about us and the things they do to us. But we need to remember that people put others down because they themselves lack self-worth. They attack others because it is less threatening than working on themselves. And this is true of people at all stages of life, from school-yard bullies to heads of corporations. I've found it in fellow actors at auditions and from directors and producers. And it isn't any more pleasant as an adult in the arts than it was as a kid in the projects of Cincinnati. I try to ignore it and work around it as much as possible, and to hitch my wagon to the many generous, hardworking, and helpful people I meet instead.

It helps in coming to terms with ourselves not to judge others too harshly and to be quick to understand and slow to condemn. It's important to get in the habit of extending those same kindnesses to ourselves. No one likes to fail, but failure is not a death sentence. Thomas Edison "failed" to invent the light bulb countless times, but he chose not to see those attempts as failures. He thought of them as steps on the road to success.

The best advice I could give is to keep the focus on yourself. Be willing to work hard to achieve your goals. Rely on yourself, but accept the help of friends. And never forget that good friends are invaluable in helping you discover who you authentically are.

FOOD FOR THOUGHT

1. When did you stick up for yourself as a child, and when did you give in to what seemed like insurmountable obstacles? How did each situation and outcome make you feel?

2. Do you remember a time when you knew something was much more important than just getting what you wanted? When a desire came from the center of your being, not just from a passing fancy?

3. How is accepting help from others a way of learning to be ourselves and getting what we know we need?

4. How does finding a group of peers help us become ourselves and trust our instincts?

5. What does it do for our fledgling sense of self to earn our own money, to buy things we want or need that we could not get any other way?

6. In what ways did you enjoy being singled out for praise and recognition, and in what ways were you terrified? How did you learn to accept that you had something to offer and to take pride in your abilities?

7. How does facing your fears and surviving make taking risks easier?

8. How does learning to trust your own instincts begin, and how do you nurture it?

Be careful of what you water your dreams with. Water them with worry and fear and you will produce weeds that choke the life from your dream. Water them with optimism and solutions and you will cultivate success. Always be on the lookout for ways to turn a problem into an opportunity for success. Always be on the lookout for ways to nurture your dream.

—Aileen Miga and Janice Hughes,
life coaches

Chapter 7

THE BIRTH
OF AN ACTOR

Investing in hard work and commitment with an attitude of service not only helps you reach your goals, it assists in acquiring the ability to delay gratification— one of the most important things we can learn, no matter what path we are on. Strong effort combined with focus can help develop and nurture your passion and reap benefits beyond your wildest dreams.

The Cincinnati School for Creative and Performing Arts has a very long name, so the students and staff simply call it SCPA or Performing Arts. SCPA goes from fourth to twelfth grade and offers training in everything from art and music to dance, stagecraft, and design. I attended SCPA from the tenth through the twelfth grade, and they were some of the best years of my life. To me, it was the most amazing school on the planet, and it served as a cultural and creative outlet for students of all races, genders, and financial backgrounds.

The SCPA school colors are black and white. This was especially appropriate, because it was rare that any production at Performing Arts was cast with leads of only one race. It was enlightening and inspiring to see black and white students cast opposite one another because their talent and commitment to the characters they were portraying were deemed more important than their ethnicities.

In those days, cast diversity was revolutionary for an ultraconservative city like Cincinnati. Color-blind casting afforded me and many other students of color wonderful opportunities that might otherwise have been closed to us. Additionally, the leads in the shows were double cast, which increased the opportunities for students to play principal roles.

Coming from Peoples Junior High, and having just had such wonderful, integrated, character-building experiences there, SCPA was the perfect next step for me on my journey of self-discovery. Performing Arts was exceedingly successful in cultivating the arts, but it took great pride in being a fine academic institution as well. The students were talented, competitive, and bright. SCPA felt more like a college than a public high school.

I will never forget my first day at SCPA. I attended an orientation session for new students the day before formal classes began. The tour guide was a young woman named Nancy. At one point, I raised my hand to ask her a question and called her "Miss." She looked at me like I was crazy and told me that, just like me, she was just starting the tenth grade. My mouth dropped open. I thought she was a teacher. Nancy had spent the morning leading a large group of us around the school on a welcome tour. She seemed so mature and confident. Later that year when I saw her play the young Helen Keller in *The Miracle Worker*, I was awestruck by her talent.

After the orientation, Nancy gave us all some great advice. She said that the school was filled with talented kids and that a lot of them were already working professionally. Sarah Jessica Parker, Carmen Electra, and Rocky Carroll of *NCIS* are all former students. She said that competition at the school was stiff; it was sink or swim. If you wanted to succeed, you needed to summon the courage to go for it and try to stand out in the best, most positive way you could.

Nancy advised me that since I was a new kid at the school, it was extra important for me to do whatever I could to get noticed. She suggested that I begin to build a reputation as a hard worker by volunteering to help in any way possible and to usher for any and all school productions. I took her advice and immediately signed up to assist and usher for every show that I could.

A requirement of volunteering was staying at school in the evenings during tech rehearsals. Tech is when a show has been staged and is ready to transfer from a rehearsal space to the theater. At this point, all lines have been memorized and the show is ready to be set up with lights, sound, and costume cues. Tech was especially tough at school because we'd had regular class all day and had to be right back for homeroom the next morning no matter how late the rehearsal lasted. Our academic teachers were only marginally concerned about how much sleep we got. They were flexible and understanding to a point, but we were expected to show up on time with our assignments completed. It was a great exercise in balance, personal responsibility, and discipline. These are tools that I still carry with me to this day.

It was during a tech rehearsal that one of the drama teachers, Mr. Stull, took notice of me. It was late one evening during rehearsals for the fourth or fifth show for which I was volunteering behind the scenes. I loved watching Mr. Stull direct. He brought an intensity and passion to his work that I found inspiring. I was one of the last students cleaning up after rehearsal when I saw him looking at me curiously from across the room. After watching me stack the last few chairs, he finally came over and asked me who I was. He asked me in a tone that suggested that he should have already known me.

I told him my name, that I was in the tenth grade, and that this was my first year at the school. "You seem to be everywhere," he said, smiling at me as though he could sense my determination. I went home that night floating on a cloud; taking Nancy's advice had paid off. Mr. Stull, one of the main directors at the school, had noticed me. Wow!

Tech rehearsals are notorious for being long, slow, and boring, but I loved every minute of them. It was during tech that I got to watch and learn from my gifted schoolmates as they rehearsed and perfected their roles. The talent at the school was astounding. Having the benefit of observing these young actors working through the process of creating a role was a master class in itself. I marveled at how they honed their craft and interacted with the directors. It was a great way for me to be of service while I slowly worked up my nerve to finally audition myself.

Every year there were three main stage musicals: one for the elementary kids, one for the junior high kids, and one for the high school students. In addition, toward the end of the year, there was one huge musical that brought all the students together. It would be a big show like *Oklahoma!* or *The Wiz*. My first year there, in 1980, that big musical was Rodgers and Hammerstein's *Carousel*.

My first audition for any show at SCPA was for *Carousel*. It brought up my usual combination of terror and excitement, but this time was different, because these auditions were held in the auditorium in front of everyone, and critiques were given for all to hear. I looked around and was stunned that no one seemed at all unsettled or intimidated about having to sing in front of the entire school. Talk about a crash course in getting over your fears.

After sitting in the auditorium watching student after student audition and trying to gather my resolve, I heard my name being called. I walked onto the stage and stated my name and my grade. I was petrified and didn't know where to focus when I sang. I knew that there was no way that I was going to look out into an audience full of my schoolmates' faces, so I looked straight ahead to the back wall and sang the required sixteen bars of "If I Loved You" from the show.

I was told that it was good, but a little heavy on the vibrato. I remember feeling relieved that I got through it but also a little disappointed in myself, because I had intentionally added extra vibrato. I thought that because I was a black kid I was expected to sound "black and soulful." I didn't trust myself enough at the time to sing the song the way that was natural for me, which was to keep it simple with an emphasis on the melody. Even though I loved all kinds of music, I knew that the music I wanted to sing was more Johnny Mathis than James Brown. In the tenth grade, I did not know or trust my vocal instrument enough to just let it flow. By the end of my time at SCPA, I had fully accepted my musical preferences and my particular aptitude for dramatic baritone anthems.

Still, my big break at SCPA came during rehearsals for *Carousel* . . . so yes, I was cast in the show! *Yaaaaaaay!*

I was in the ensemble of my first show at the Cincinnati School for Creative and Performing Arts, and I was too excited for words. After months of staying late after school, ushering, helping clean the theater after performances, and watching other students work, I was actually onstage myself.

Senior year at Performing Arts was a particularly huge deal for students. When *Carousel* was announced as the big end-of-year show, every senior musical theater major dreamed of getting one of the lead roles in their final performance at the school. One of the seniors I admired from afar was terribly upset, however, that he had not been cast as Billy Bigelow, the carnival barker who is at the center of the plot. The student, Gary, was tall, dark, and very handsome. He looked like a black Cary Grant. I idolized him because he seemed so suave and confident, and was always so well-dressed. He carried himself with a kind of confidence that I hoped to have myself someday. He was an incredibly talented and intense actor, but unfortunately, singing was not his strong suit. He had been cast as the Captain instead and, because of his disappointment, he never came to rehearsals. So, though it's one of the dramatic highlights of the show, we always had to skip over the Captain's scene after Billy dies.

A few days before we were to begin tech, the cast was onstage doing the scene leading up to it when our director, Mr. Stull, blew up about Gary being absent yet again. He stormed out of the theater and everything came to a standstill. After a few minutes, the director returned and hung out in the back of the auditorium, pacing and conversing feverishly with Mr. Louiso, the artistic director of the school. I was onstage chatting with my good friend Andra, who was also a member of the chorus. He was convinced that they were looking my way and talking about me. I shrugged it off until the two teachers started pointing directly at me. And then, just like in the movies, Mr. Stull's voice rang out: "Hey you, kid. Come here."

Mr. Stull led me out of the theater and across the hall to the main office, then handed me a piece of paper. It was the Captain's scene, where he gives orders to those around him about what to do after Billy Bigelow has died. He told me to read the scene with him and afterward asked me if I thought I could handle it. I said yes, and just like that, I went from a chorus member to a principal role. I was over the moon! Mr. Stull said that the company was going to be on a break for the next few minutes, and I asked if I could please use one of the office phones to call my mother with the great news.

He smiled, congratulated me, and left the office. When my mother picked up I nearly screamed in her ear, I was so excited. She was absolutely thrilled for me and told me how proud of me she was.

The entire experience of my first show onstage at SCPA, from rehearsals through to the performances, was amazing. In addition to full company rehearsals, there were more intimate ones where only the principals or leads were called to work. I actually missed the first one of these because I didn't realize at the time that my part was considered a principal one. The smaller rehearsals were even more informative than those for the whole cast. I reveled in watching the director work one-on-one with the actors and really break down the scenes to tap into deeper meaning and intention. I learned so much, and it was enormously gratifying to see my hard work, patience, willingness, and perseverance pay off.

SCPA exposed me to so many wonderful aspects of art and creativity that I could never describe them all. Every year, the entire school went on field trips to the Cincinnati Music Hall for operas, ballets, and orchestral concerts, and to the Cincinnati Playhouse in the Park to see professional New York actors perform what are called "legit" plays. I always loved the question-and-answer periods afterward when we were allowed to ask the actors about being professional artists.

It was while attending SCPA that I was cast in my very first opera, *Amahl and the Night Visitors*. The Cincinnati Opera came to the school for auditions, and I was cast as the Page for a local tour performing in the tristate area (Ohio, Kentucky, and Indiana). I was ecstatic to have booked my first professional theater job. I got paid, I got to travel, and I got to take time off from school. I only had to miss a few days, but it was exciting to be working in the arts and then go back to class to make up my assignments with such a great excuse.

SENIOR YEAR

My senior year at SCPA was wonderful and transformative. For my first play, I was cast in Herb Gardner's *Thieves* as Martin, the male lead; then *The King and I* was chosen as the big musical of the 1981–82 school year. Because the competition was so stiff, SCPA made the rare decision to triple cast the lead roles. I was cast as one of the three kings (not to be confused with the three kings of *Amahl and the Night Visitors*) and then, even better, I was singled out to be featured in a televised special about the school.

The program was split into five segments that aired on the local ABC news affiliate for a week. A few weeks later, a half-hour compilation version was broadcast. The crew spent an entire day following me around from class to class and even rode the bus home with me to interview my mother. In addition, the crew was also present to film all three of the student kings of Siam when we got our heads shaved for the first time.

Meanwhile, there were also big changes occurring at home. By this time my parents had separated, and during my senior year, my mother and I moved out of the projects into an amazing triplex apartment in Price Hill on the newly racially mixed west side of town. Before we moved there, I had only visited that neighborhood once before.

Similar to when I had attended Peoples Junior High in Hyde Park, moving to Price Hill brought me to a very different world and gave me another opportunity to discover and reinvent myself. I was ecstatic that so many of my dreams were coming together after what had often seemed like such impossible odds. I had long outgrown my surroundings, and moving away from the projects allowed me to learn about a different part of Cincinnati and continue to express myself more fully without the physical baggage and everyday reminders of my childhood misery.

Since it was now just the two of us, my mother and I became closer, and both of our lives changed pretty dramatically. With me as the only kid in the house—and earning my own money during the summers—my mother's finances were no longer stretched as thin as they had been all her life. We went from barely making ends meet to living a more middle-class existence in an amazing modern apartment with spectacular views of downtown, the Ohio River, and northern Kentucky beyond. Suddenly, my life was more like that TV existence I'd seen and fantasized about when I was growing up.

We had come a long way from the overcrowded space of many years before—from my sleeping on the floor in the hallway to having my own room, my own bathroom, and my own phone line. When I got my driver's license at sixteen, my mother let me take her brand-new Ford Mustang out with friends and on weekend dates. At seventeen, I had my first-ever birthday party for friends, because I was no longer embarrassed about my living situation. My world had opened up completely, and I could not have been more grateful.

Even though my mother and I now had more time to spend together, she still knew very little about my life at school. I had gotten so used to taking care of myself, to the dualities in my life, and to feeling like I was always in everyone's way at home that I seldom shared details about myself with my mom or my family.

A perfect example was the opening night of *The King and I*. Of the three casts, mine was chosen to open the run. It was an exceptionally big deal because of all the press coverage surrounding the school after the telecast on the local TV station. At the curtain call, my performance was met with a rousing standing ovation, and the camera crew was backstage to film my exit from the stage. Teachers, creative staff, and castmates all crowded into the dressing room to congratulate me on my performance, and then the principal asked me if I'd like someone to get my family from the audience and bring them back to see me. I will never forget the look of utter shock and disbelief on his face when I told him that none of my family was at the performance. He could not fathom that I had no family members present to witness such a momentous event in my life. With all the coverage that led up the show, my family knew that it was happening, but none of them had expressed any interest in coming to the show.

To be honest, I wasn't concerned about their absence. It was more important to me that I was happy. I felt accepted. I was expressing myself in ways I hadn't had the courage to even face before. And I was doing what I loved.

A HINT OF THE FUTURE

Another major event during my senior year of high school was going to see the movie *Ragtime*. I wasn't familiar with E. L. Doctorow's wildly popular historical novel, which won the National Book Critics Circle Award for fiction in 1975, but a huge, highly publicized deal was made when the story came to the screen in 1981. Plus, having Howard Rollins, then an unknown black actor, in the lead made me both curious and eager to see it. As it turned out, the film completely knocked me out. It was an experience that changed my perception of life as I had previously known it.

The main character of *Ragtime*, Coalhouse Walker Jr., is a perfect example of a hardworking, gifted black man trying to recover from the devastation of slavery and oppression and find his way in America at the begin-ning of a new century. Coalhouse is proud of his power and skill as a musician. He meets and woos his love,

117

Sarah, who becomes pregnant and runs away because she fears that he will not settle down and become a responsible husband and father to their child. To prove his devotion to her, Coalhouse exercises the discipline and willingness to mature and puts forth a tireless effort in pursuit of her, hoping to convince Sarah and the family that she is staying with that he is deserving of her. He is so convincing that the family yearns to have the couple reunited as much as he does.

Coalhouse's talent, character, commitment, and discipline are what afford him a brand-new Ford Model T to carry his future wife and child down the road of opportunity in what he thought was the new America. While passing through a small town on the way to visit his family, Coalhouse is harassed and his car is defaced by envious white townsfolk who cannot abide a Negro with such a beautiful new piece of machinery. He is stunned and insulted because he had worked so hard to follow all the unwritten rules regarding pursuing the American dream. His courage and passion for justice throughout the entire story are riveting.

When I saw Howard Rollins on-screen as Coalhouse Walker Jr., I was mesmerized. I had never seen a black male actor of my generation portray a strong character with such a particular blend of strength and defenselessness. The range of emotions that Rollins displayed to depict the multifaceted character's complex struggle was phenomenal. His combination of passion, pain, and strength was unlike anything I had seen. Watching him on-screen felt like witnessing grown-up aspects of my own childhood. As a young survivor of many unpleasant things, I had learned to turn some of my adversities into strengths, so I strongly identified not only with Coalhouse, but also with the actor who played him.

I had not heard of Howard Rollins before *Ragtime*, but there was something eerily recognizable about him. Even with all the power and confidence he exuded, I could sense an all-too-familiar suffering and vulnerability beneath it. Later, I discovered that Howard Rollins battled substance abuse problems for many years before his death at age forty-six in 1996. I don't know if Howard grew up in an environment of alcohol and drug abuse, but in interviews, he struck me as someone who had suffered devastating circumstances early in his life. I felt a deep connection to both the actor and his character.

After seeing this extraordinary man in a life-changing film, I knew that, against all odds, I *had* to be an actor. This realization frightened me more than it excited me, because I didn't know how I'd ever get out of Cincinnati, let alone make it as a professional actor. *Ragtime* would prove to be a powerful vehicle for change later in my life.

Inspiration comes in many forms and it is in your best interest to be present and courageous enough to be open to receive them. If allowed, inspiration can open doors and lead you down successful paths that may have seemed impossible before.

The lore of theater is full of chorus members who had to go on for the star and became even bigger stars themselves. But that's because those chorus members knew the lead's part. They had talent and they had honed their craft. They had studied singing, dancing, and acting. They had also worked hard and cheerfully in their chorus roles, and had proven their professionalism by showing up on time, being ready to work, and leaving their personal drama at the stage door. We hear of these stars because they were prepared. *They did their work and were happy to have it. They gave their assigned roles their all, and it paid off. If an unknown member of the chorus had stepped into the lead's part and forgotten her lyrics or her dance steps or her lines, we would never have heard of her again. If you resent not being the "star," in whatever profession you choose, chances are you will never be one.*

Life is also full of stories of people who were headed happily down path A when path B presented itself, and they took an opportunity that changed their lives forever. Until I had the chance to act and to perform in musical theater, my fantasies were primarily about singing. Now, singing to acting is not as major a shift as, say, botanist to race car driver, but it was a different path than I had planned on taking.

Living in the now is also key. "I want to go down path A, but someone is inviting me to go down path B. I may not like path B, but . . . I don't have to choose for all time. I only have to choose in this moment. I can try path B and see if I like the fit. If not, I can choose again later." By giving path B your very best effort, you might find a new life. If not, it's not a tragedy.

Very few things are actually impossible. They may seem impossible, but consider the following: Helen Keller, a blind and deaf girl, learned to read and write and eventually graduated from college, the first deaf-blind person ever to receive a bachelor's degree—and from Radcliffe College at Harvard University. Rick Allen, the drummer for Def Leppard, has only one arm. And you can be sure that more than one person told Barack Obama it was not possible for a black man to be elected president of the United States. Be realistic, but dream beyond your comfort zone, because that's where passion lies.

FOOD FOR THOUGHT

1. Can you remember ever being recognized for volunteer work and having it lead to something more? Have you ever been promoted for doing a humble task well?

2. How can being prepared be the secret to success?

3. How can our emotional reactions to what we are doing in our lives help us understand the concept of following our passion?

4. What does it take to reinvent yourself while maintaining your authentic core? How is it possible to change but stay essentially true to yourself?

5. Have you ever been excluded or demeaned for being "different," whether it's for being a member of a minority or for your behavior, physical characteristics, or economic status? How is it possible to overcome this kind of treatment?

Competing at the highest level is not about winning. It's about preparation, courage, understanding and nurturing your people, and heart. Winning is the result.

—Joe Torre, baseball player and manager

Chapter 8

TO COLLEGE
AND BEYOND

You may not know how you're going to get there, and you may doubt it will ever happen, but ultimately all you can do is be prepared and available. Remember, it is fundamental to nurture your courage and spirit and keep asking the higher source within you. How? Continuously asking the question creates openings and mental paths toward reaching your goals.

I graduated from the Cincinnati School for Creative and Performing Arts on Saturday, June 5, 1982. The ceremony at the city's celebrated Music Hall marked an ending to a magical period of my life where so many of my fantasies had come true, and my dreams had begun to seem like possibilities. SCPA had been the haven where I came out of my shell of self-consciousness and expressed myself as an artist.

As it happened, Rob North, the newscaster who had hosted the TV special about my work in *The King and I* at Performing Arts, was the commencement speaker. In his speech, he praised the school and then singled me out to predict that I was the "most likely to succeed" in our class. The crowd rose to cheer. I actually got a standing ovation at my high school graduation!

I remember sitting there astonished. My mind raced back to three years earlier when I had first come to the school, scared to death and afraid to show who I really was, but thankful that I had enough personality to mask my shyness and hidden anxieties. Back then I'd known only a few people at the school, and now I was being celebrated at graduation.

A few months before graduation, just before I turned eighteen, I was cast as a featured performer at the Cascade Cabaret, a new dinner theater venue that was the talk of the town in Cincinnati. Cascade was extremely accommodating regarding my school schedule, and we performed only on the weekends. I loved being in the show and was so dedicated that instead of taking the night off for my senior prom, I brought my date to the performance, threw on my tux, and raced over to the event just in time to be crowned prom king—much to my surprise.

I could never have imagined such a triumphant end to my high school years. In three unbelievably full and gratifying adolescent years, I had changed dramatically from a tentative, quiet kid into a more open, mature, and self-assured young man whose personality had begun to really blossom. I was grateful, happy, and amazed all at the same time.

I was also keenly aware on that very day that I still hadn't made any solid plans for the future. I had not yet learned that "living in the now" did not preclude laying the groundwork for what I hoped would happen next.

I longed to pursue the arts, but it didn't seem practical, so to get my head back into the "real world," I applied to Ohio University in Athens, Ohio, to study business. I had spent most of my senior year in a kind of blissful denial that high school would eventually end and that my fantasy life would be over. Toward the end of the last semester I finally snapped out of it enough to apply to only one college.

My mother and father had separated, but the two of them drove me to Athens for registration. My mother was nervous, excited, and also sad that I was moving away from home for the first time. Still, both my parents were pleased that I was going to college. I remember sitting in the back seat feeling that what I was doing was the *sensible* thing, but knowing in my gut that it was not the right thing for me. I had family and friends who were counting on me to succeed. I felt the weight of my family's pride and their great expectations for me, but I couldn't shake the inner conflict I felt about abandoning my dream of being a performer. This was not a struggle I could easily shake.

I thought that once I got to Ohio University, I'd be able to tap back into the more studious version of myself from before Performing Arts, when my life was almost exclusively academic. The conflict was particularly difficult for me because I was intellectually curious and had always enjoyed learning. I hoped that once I was on campus and with other academic students, I'd fall back into that mind-set. I sat in the back seat praying this would be true.

We arrived at Ohio University and unloaded my things into my dorm room. Then I walked my parents back to the car to say goodbye. My father told me to take care of myself and that he was very proud of me. My mother burst into tears, kissed and hugged me, and told me how proud she was, too. I stood there watching them until the car was out of sight, just as panic started to set in. It was a feeling of overwhelming isolation, watching my parents drive away, knowing that I was about to enter a world that didn't excite me *at all*. In fact, I was dreading it.

Being at Ohio University was challenging from the start. Being back in a nonartistic environment was much more difficult than I had anticipated. Everywhere I went I heard music. I tried to ignore its siren call. After the first week of classes, just for fun, I gave in and inquired about what kind of artistic programs were available on campus. The only thing I found that fit my schedule was a dance class that met twice a week in the late afternoon. Before the end of the first class, all I could think of was how much I missed the arts. By the third week of the fall semester, I looked forward to those two dance classes more than any of my academic ones.

Before high school, I had fantasized about going away to college, meeting new people, and having fun at campus parties. When I finally got there, I wasn't interested in meeting people who weren't creative and artistic. When I wasn't in that dance class, I felt lonely and bored. In that short amount of time, I could feel the old shy version of myself creeping back in—and I didn't like it. I had come so far in finding my voice and the courage to express myself, and now I was beginning to grow apprehensive. I felt that I was stunting my personal growth and retreating into myself.

I didn't want to disappoint my family and friends, but I also knew that I couldn't sustain the masquerade. I had already gotten "the call" of the stage. I was living a complete lie by pretending I could ever work in an office. But how on earth could I explain these feelings to anyone? How could I survive on the "impractical," unknown creative path with my feelings as my only guide? How would I live and thrive if I couldn't make plans with any sense of control over their outcome? And how would I explain this to my parents when I didn't fully understand it myself?

Attending Performing Arts had been fun, and I'd had the foundation of the school to keep me grounded, but how would I proceed in the so-called real world? What kind of life would there be for me as a black male performer? Only one of my sisters had gone off to college, to Ohio State. She'd lasted a couple of years. And though it felt like an eternity, I was ready to leave after *three weeks*. I didn't know what I was going to do or how I was going to do it, but I knew that I couldn't stay in school, not this school.

I was petrified of telling my parents, ashamed about disappointing everyone, and absolutely certain that I could not hold my breath at Ohio University for a fourth week, let alone four more years.

Over the next few days following my epiphany, I cried enough tears to fill a swimming pool. But I finally came up with a plan. My instincts told me to first call Bev Harpeneau, my former boss from the Cascade Cabaret. It was an embarrassing call to make, because the cast had just thrown me a big going-away celebration just weeks before, and already I was planning to come back home.

She asked me how things were going, and I told her this: not great. Her next question was exactly what I wanted to hear. "Would you like to come back to the show?" she asked. I said yes before she finished the question. I told her that I missed performing and that I didn't know how I was going to make a living doing it but that I had to try. She asked what my parents thought about how I felt. I told her that I had not told them yet and that I thought having a job to come home to would soften the blow.

Bev assured me that I was very talented and that the cast and the show had missed my presence and performance. But she further stressed the importance of being authentic with myself first and then sharing my honest feelings with my family. She said to let her know how things turned out and that I had her and the company's support, whatever I decided. I thought deeply about my chat with Bev for about an hour before making the call home.

When my mother picked up the phone, her mama instincts kicked in immediately and she asked me what was wrong. I told her that things weren't working out at school, that I was unhappy, and that I couldn't stay. She took a deep breath, and then she asked me what I was going to do, and more importantly, what I really *wanted* to do. I could hear the worry in her voice as I told her that I wanted to be a performer. I told her that I had talked to my old boss at the Cascade and that I could have my job back in the show.

I assured her of my plan to move back home, go back to work in the show, contribute financially to the household, and register for general studies at the University of Cincinnati. My mother asked me when I wanted to come back home, and I told her ASAP. The following weekend my parents were back to help me reload the car to take me "home" to Cincinnati.

After I unpacked, my mother came into my room to talk. And then she gave me the best advice I've ever received. She said, "Alton, if you are going to be a professional entertainer, then do it. Don't rely on the 'all black folks can sing and dance' nonsense. Go to school and study and learn so that you can be the best at it. Don't be a part-time entertainer and part-time something else. If this is what you choose, then commit to it and make being the best at it your primary focus." Many times over the years, in moments of deep doubt about what I was doing with my life in my pursuit of the arts, this stunningly sage advice from my mother sustained me.

To be sure, it was embarrassing to come back home, but the joy of being back onstage and the feeling of contentment from following my instincts far outweighed the shame. The next semester I registered at the University of Cincinnati in general studies and set my sights on getting myself into the school's prized College-Conservatory of Music (CCM).

CCM was one of the top musical theater schools in the country, and although it, like Performing Arts, was in my hometown, there was a perception that it rarely accepted students from our school. One of the exceptions was a student named Darrell Miller who graduated from Performing Arts a year ahead of me.

At that time, there were a record three black men in the Musical Theatre department at CCM: Darrell; Donald Lawrence, who is now a Grammy-winning gospel artist; and Rufus Bonds Jr., who would later become one of my first mentors. Having three black men in the department was revolutionary at that time.

Twice a year at CCM, musical theater students had to perform what were called "boards" or "juries." Students had to sing two contrasting songs in front of a panel of the directors of the program. It was a big deal on campus, because they were open to every student in the school to see. A lot of the non-theater students on campus viewed the juries as a free ticket to the best show in town.

Darrell wanted to do a piece from *The Wiz* as one of his two songs, perhaps because there were finally enough black performers on campus. He asked me if I would play the Scarecrow. I said yes immediately. Of course, I knew that in addition to being a great favor for him, it would be a great audition/introduction to the Musical Theatre department at CCM as well.

The performance was received extremely well, and afterward I was introduced to the head of the department. He complimented me on my work and asked if I'd be interested in applying for the department. Flattered and thrilled, I said yes as modestly and calmly as possible.

I auditioned for the artistic faculty a few weeks later

and was accepted as a musical theater major for the beginning of the next school year.

KINGS ISLAND SUMMER

I was, of course, beyond excited to be accepted by the Musical Theatre department and eager to begin classes in the fall. I was ready to get back to studying musical theater full time. The summer before classes started, I had the good fortune of booking a dream job as a featured performer at one of my favorite childhood places in the world, Kings Island amusement park.

For many years, my sister Marcia (my sister pronounced it Mar-see-a) worked at Procter and Gamble, and every summer the company bought out the whole park for Procter and Gamble Day. When she got passes, she invited me to tag along with her and her family. It was the highlight of my summers, because I *love* roller coasters. To this day, Kings Island still has The Beast, the longest roller coaster in the United States and the longest wooden roller coaster in the world.

Everything about the theme park experience was happy, fun, and exciting to me. That annual visit to the park made up for all the dull summer days I'd endured in my neighborhood being teased, terrorized, or left to play all by myself.

I don't recall ever going as a family to any of the live musical shows at Kings Island, because no one else in the family was interested, but I'd always catch any glimpses that I could of the outdoor shows. There were several of them throughout the park, but the main stage show was indoors at the American Heritage Theater (now the Kings Island Theater). Many summers, when I passed the building, I experienced a mixture of sensations: I found it thrilling, intimidating, and intriguing all at the same time.

I finally got up enough nerve to break away from the family and go to one of the shows. I was blown away by what I saw—a huge Broadway-style show with big floating set pieces, smoke on the stage, beautiful costumes, colorful lighting, and incredible singing and dancing. I left the show mesmerized and in disbelief that I'd seen something so fantastic and glamorous in Cincinnati.

The summer before I began classes at CCM, Kings Island was auditioning singers and dancers for a brand-new show called *Gotta Dance*. The show was packed with a wide range of music and dance styles, from old Hollywood musicals to rap and pop. Performing consistently at the Cascade Cabaret had built up my confidence, so, thankfully, my audition jitters had significantly decreased. Less than a year after leaving Ohio University, I'd been accepted at CCM, and now I was about to have a wonderful new summer adventure, performing at a place that I already loved so much.

During the first few days of rehearsal, the musical director had the singers learn all the songs to prepare

135

for auditioning for the solo spots in the production. The songs ranged from "Puttin' on the Ritz" and "Singin' in the Rain" to "Flashdance," "Footloose," and "Thriller," by my boyhood idol, Michael Jackson. The company of singers and dancers would be split into three casts: A, B, and C. It took two casts to complete a show, which meant that every performance day, there'd be a different combination of performers. For instance, if you were a performer in the A cast, on an A-B day, you might have one performing track, and on an A-C day, you might have a completely different performing track.

After a few days, the cast list was posted. When I saw it, my mouth literally dropped open. I had been assigned to the A cast and was given every male solo in the show, including a featured male dance solo. This meant that on my A-B days, I did half of all the male solos, and on my A-C days, I did the other half (in addition to the featured dance number). I was thrilled and a bit overwhelmed, because out of all of the singers in the cast, I was one of the new kids on the block. I put my fears aside, focused on my gratitude for having this great opportunity, and dug right in.

Rehearsals were fast and furious, but I loved every single minute of them. I was finally doing what I really wanted to do and getting paid well for it! Tech rehearsals for *Gotta Dance* were intense. Performing a high-energy show with enormous sets that quickly transitioned from one to the next was daunting. I had to figure out how to make speedy costume changes between back-to-back solos. For many of the scenes, the stage was filled with smoke from dry ice, making me feel like I was in a classic musical film or already starring in a Broadway show.

Shortly after the performances began, I gained a following of fans who saw the show over and over and waited at the stage door for autographs. My number one fan was a young girl named Jennifer. Her enthusiasm and words of encouragement were inspiring. She is still a good friend and great cheerleader of mine.

That summer at Kings Island was one of the most fun summers of my life. We performed five shows a day several times a week, and I loved it. Every day I felt blessed and validated, relieved and vindicated that leaving Ohio University had been the right thing to do.

MR. WHITE IN THE CONSERVATORY; OR, BE CAREFUL WHAT YOU WISH FOR

I couldn't wait to begin classes and continue my training in the arts at CCM. I'd learned a lot in my three years at Performing Arts and as a paid professional performer, and I was excited to take those experiences to a higher level. Ultimately, though, my time at CCM would prove to be three years of difficultly and pain. Unfortunately, it took me two and a half of those years to figure out what was really going on.

The biannual juries turned out to be a particular problem for me. If you fail two of them, you are let go from the department. Of the six juries I performed while at CCM, the department failed me on all but one. Each failure was a "conditional failure," meaning that I wouldn't be kicked out of the department but that there was still a lot of work that I needed to do. I was told that I would have to present an extra board sometime during the year to rectify the failure; yet every time I tried to set up an appointment to do so, it was postponed. The "conditional failures" were confusing to me. My professors didn't provide any specific criticisms or specific tools to remedy or mollify their disapprovals. I was on edge attending a school that didn't seem to accept me or take the time to understand or nurture me.

For most of my boards, I would choose traditional musical theater songs like scenes and selections from Rodgers and Hammerstein musicals. I was told that I picked too many pretty songs that showed off my voice and that they already knew that I could do that. They said that they weren't seeing enough growth and that I needed to present songs that had more contrast and more of an edge. No one on the juries gave me suggestions or examples as to what kinds of songs they thought might be better.

For my next board, I picked the most contrasting songs that I could find: "Maria" from *West Side Story*—sweeping, beautiful, and romantic—and "The Viper's Drag (The Reefer

Song)," a slinky, overtly sexual and humorous number about smoking weed that helped make André De Shields a Broadway legend in *Ain't Misbehavin'*. I performed "Maria" in a long overcoat and stood in the center of the stage, delivering it as simply and directly as I could, making sure to play the honesty of the lyrics and the sincerity of the character.

For "The Viper's Drag," I lost the overcoat and donned a black bowler hat that matched my tight black leotard and tank top. I'd spent hours in a studio by myself choreographing a corresponding routine, using an unlit cigarette in place of a joint. I chose "Maria" because *West Side Story* is one of my favorite musicals and "The Viper's Drag" because *Ain't Misbehavin'* was a Tony- and Grammy-winning all-black musical that I loved. (Just a few months later, I was cast in the role of Andre at Cincinnati's Showboat Majestic to fantastic reviews.)

After my jury presentation, I received a standing ovation. Afterward, I sat with my classmates and waited for the auditorium to empty as we prepared to have the meeting with our professors where they critiqued our work. My classmates were excited for me because it seemed like I'd finally cracked the code.

The instructors saved me for last. Then they unloaded. My critiques were unanimously negative. Several of them said that they were shocked by what they'd just seen me do and that they didn't think that I was "that kind of person," which to me could be translated as many things, none of them good or politically correct. The head professor was the last to speak. He looked at me, let out an exasperated sigh, shook his head as if he'd just about had enough, and said, "I have no idea what you just did up there. I don't even know what to say to you." He seemed appalled by my performance and offered me yet another "conditional failure."

My classmates let out audible gasps, and I was simply too stunned to even react.

I left the auditorium feeling like I'd just been kicked in the stomach. For the past three years, I had tried so hard to follow their instructions, and now I was running out of solutions. Just a few years before, I'd had the starring role in *The King and I* at Performing Arts, yet at CCM, I was not cast in a single show. Every summer between school years, I would work at Kings Island as a soloist, then come back to CCM and be made to feel like I didn't know what I was doing.

I felt isolated from my classmates. I tried to bond with them as much as I could, but I was the only student in my class who didn't live on campus, which was a major social disadvantage, even if being able to live with my mother in my hometown did save me a great deal of money. I was blessed to have a seasonal job at Kings Island, but had it not for been that, I would have needed to work somewhere else. I was paying for my own education, with some financial aid, so I needed to work and couldn't afford to live on campus. I felt alone, confused, and stressed, and the department heads seemed incapable of understanding or helping me.

I didn't know what I should do. My instincts were telling me to get out of there, but the thought of leaving yet another school was terrifying. I tried very hard to be strong, but I didn't know how much longer I could hold my head above water in what felt like a stagnant, discouraging environment.

The tipping point for me came when I saw two of my professors later on the afternoon of my "Maria"/ "Viper's Drag" jury presentation. I ran into each of them separately. Both of them pulled me aside and congratulated me on my performance. Two of the same professors who'd slammed me only hours before were now complimenting me on how daring and courageous my performance had been. It became clear to me that even though they approved of my performance, the head professor had the final say, and they all had to fall in line with him.

I spent that weekend in my room confused and depressed. I didn't share any of this with my mother because I didn't want to worry her. I'd tried my very best to make leaving Ohio University worth it, and I didn't want to upset and disappoint her again. The past three years had been a struggle because, as much as I wanted to get good training, I knew in my gut that after my first summer working at Kings Island, I was ready to be a full-time working actor. But I was afraid to take the leap of faith.

By the end of that weekend I had figured it out. At Performing Arts, Cascade Cabaret, and Kings Island, I had gotten great training and work experience before I'd even started college. CCM seemed to favor students who were "fresh off the farm." Most of them had very little experience, and it was hard to pretend that I didn't already have a great deal. The biggest realization for me was that the professors at CCM didn't know what to do with me because I was a black male.

I was a young black man with talent and experience but with nowhere for them to place me. I even had one professor go around the room, student by student, to discuss who she thought would be the "right type" for different Broadway shows. When she got to me, she stopped and said it was unfortunate that all that was waiting for me in theater were slave-type roles like Joe in *Show Boat*. She said this quite apologetically but in front of my whole class nonetheless.

My immediate thought was that her mistaken perception was not my future reality. I didn't disagree aloud or comment on what she said in class that day. I just looked her dead in the eye, expressionless.

The wonderful model of color-blind casting at SCPA had given me the confidence to pursue any role and to approach it with assurance, undistracted by the character's ethnicity. That kind of opportunity would never be available to me at the exalted CCM. Over that weekend, after crying my eyes out, my gut told me that no matter how talented I was or how hard I worked, being cast in a lead role at CCM would never happen for me.

Working through my feelings, looking back on my history, and coming to that realization were a tremendous relief. It suddenly made some sense why I had been given the runaround, why nothing I did seemed to move me forward in the department. Just as they had before I left Ohio University, my instincts told me that my days at CCM were numbered. I didn't know what was next for me, but from that point on, instead of trying to please my professors, I made the decision to tailor the program to fit my own needs as long as I was there.

I would continue to take classes, do my best, and focus on what they had to offer. I would leave the rest of it behind. I had a new sense of freedom and personal validation, which allowed for a healthy sense of detachment from the department, making the environment less toxic for me.

Kings Island did the same show for two consecutive summers and then premiered a new one. Their next show was *Fascinating Rhythm*. After having performed all the male solos in *Gotta Dance* for two summers, I auditioned to be the male vocal swing because I needed the extra challenge. My discipline and strong work ethic there paid off and resulted in another of my dreams coming true: traveling and singing with a live band.

Kings Productions, the owners of Kings Island and the producers of its shows, had several parks throughout the country. At the end of every summer, they invited performers from their parks to go out on one of two USO tours to entertain US troops overseas. The competition was stiff because hundreds of performers were competing for fourteen positions or fewer. Being offered one of those few coveted slots was the crowning achievement of a performer working for Kings Productions. One of the tours went to Europe with eight singers performing to prerecorded music; the other went to the Far East with one male soloist, three female singers, and a live three-piece band. After my third summer, I was invited to do the latter tour as the only male soloist. It was the tour that I'd always dreamed of doing. I got to travel around Asia for three glorious months. It was my first time ever being away from Ohio for more than a week and my first time flying abroad. I applied for a leave of absence from school to do it, and it was just the break from CCM that I needed.

Touring Korea, Japan, the Philippines, Guam, and Hawaii, as well as other beautiful locations in Asia and around the Pacific, opened my eyes and changed my life. In addition to performing our two-act show, we had to unload the truck, set up all the equipment, perform for the troops, and then break it all back down and reload the van. It was hard work with long hours, but the entire experience was invaluable.

I returned to Cincinnati from the tour with a month off before the next semester began at CCM. Since I had grown used to performing almost daily at this point, I was looking for something creative to get into for the rest of my time away from CCM. I reached out to one of my ex-castmates from the Cascade Cabaret. She introduced me to an amazing dance teacher named Bruce Stegmann, who taught Gus Giordano's technique. Bruce and I hit it off immediately, and he thought that I'd be a great fit for Gus's dance company in Chicago.

Chicago, even more than New York, was a city I'd visualized living in ever since I had visited it on a class trip. I loved that Chicago had a thriving theater community and that it was in the Midwest, less than four hours from Cincinnati. As much as I loved doing theater and hoped for Broadway someday, I wasn't yet ready to make the big leap to the Big Apple.

I tried very hard to get excited about going back to CCM, but I was dreading it. I showed up for classes, and by the end of my first week back, after hearing the same old song from my professors, I knew it was a wrap. I had experienced a great taste of life as an artist performing and traveling around the world, and now there was no turning back. I went home and had another difficult conversation with my mother. Then I called Bruce and asked him when auditions would be held in Chicago for Gus Giordano's dance scholarships. The auditions were a few weeks away, so I went into intense preparation by enrolling in lots of Bruce's dance classes, which were invaluable. I then rented a car, drove to Chicago, and auditioned for a scholarship at Gus Giordano Jazz Dance Chicago.

A few days later, I got a call from Nan Giordano, Gus's daughter, saying that not only had I been awarded a full scholarship, but that they had work for me as well. Several of their corporate clients had been at the auditions looking for dancers for some upcoming industrial dance shows, and they wanted to hire me for some of them. It was spectacular news! I had a full scholarship and work waiting for me in a city that I had dreamed of living in. As scary as it was to leave CCM, I knew that it was the right thing to do.

I worked at Kings Island that last summer and saved every penny I made so that I could move to Chicago and take my career beyond the limits of Cincinnati, Ohio.

A deep-seated belief in yourself may seem to come naturally to some people. My experience is that achieving some respect for yourself and committing to yourself in a deep way is one of the hardest things in the world, and that everyone who has it has struggled for it. It's also not necessarily a done deal once you've experienced it. Some of the best and hardest-working actors I know are sure they won't ever work again when their current gig is over. Belief in yourself and faith in your instincts guide you to take risks or change directions.

I have a lot of faith in my gut. My "gut" is a catch-all word for a complex of ideas and feelings. It includes my physical reactions to things as well as my emotional or psychological reactions. It includes instinct, but it is informed by experience and education. It embraces the specifics of my own life's work but extends to observation of all areas of human behavior. Spirituality is part of it, along with the relationship between myself and the universe, and the balance of all these things orbiting around each other like an inner galaxy.

I don't know if any of us "master" what I mean when I say "my gut," or if it can be mastered. I know it took a long time to develop in me and that it continues to evolve. But I knew something was wrong at CCM before my mind figured out what it was. I knew I was in the wrong place and that I had to leave. I felt that my survival depended on it. Leaving after three years might have been a disastrous step leading directly to failure, but my years of inching forward in both my craft and my courage to face adversity along with success helped me trust that feeling. And today, I know when a message is coming from my gut and when it is coming from a spasm of self-doubt.

FOOD FOR THOUGHT

1. How does it feel to do what you really think you should be doing with your life? How does it feel to do something else? Does the word "harmony" apply?

2. Has it ever been hard for you to choose the road "less traveled," as poet Robert Frost put it? Does it have anything to do with feelings of being different, and being ostracized for your difference?

3. What is unique about working in a job you are passionate about?

4. What can we do to maintain our self-confidence and self-esteem when authority figures tell us that we are not good enough?

5. How do we know when to stay put and when to move on? How can fear keep us from taking a "leap of faith"? How can relying on our "inner voice" give us courage?

One important key to success is self-confidence. An important key to self-confidence is preparation.

—Arthur Ashe, tennis star

Chapter 9

MY KIND OF TOWN, CHICAGO IS!

Following your dreams comes at a price, and there are no shortcuts to paying your dues, so practice patience, gratitude, and humility, because they will help you over the high hurdles. The rewards are knowledge, experience, and wisdom, which will be yours to access for the rest of your life!

I was twenty-one and my dream of living in Chicago was actually coming true. That summer I bought a 1980 Renault Encore hatchback, packed it up with all my things, and headed up I-74 toward Illinois. I loved Chicago's architecture and that it had a faster pace than Cincinnati, yet it was still Midwestern in outlook as well as location. To me Chicago had a sophisticated, big-city feel similar to New York—but not as intimidating.

Tajma, a CCM classmate who was from the Chicago

area, introduced me to her parents, who lived in Deerfield, about thirty miles north of Chicago. We hit it off, and they invited me to stay in a room at their house until I found a place of my own. It was exciting to be living in a thriving metropolis with the opportunity to spread my wings as a young adult.

It took me less than a month to find my own apartment in the city, in Rogers Park on the north side of town. It was a block away from Lake Michigan and the 'L' train, and only a couple of stops away from the dance studio in Evanston—a town just north of the Windy City.

I was superexcited to begin my training at Gus Giordano's. Up to that point, I was considered a "triple threat," a good singer, dancer, and actor. But dance was the discipline I had studied the least. Thankfully I had a great memory, could move well, and seemed to have a genetic sense of showmanship. What I lacked in technical skill, I made up for in picking up choreography quickly and "selling it" onstage. At Giordano's I was able to get a much-needed foundation in technique.

The class schedule at Giordano's studio was intense, because scholarship students were required to put in work time at the studio on top of taking a minimum number of classes each day. The program was strict, and it was made clear that we were to focus on studying and to hold off on auditioning for outside projects for at least a year. Because I needed to earn money while I was studying, I had to "dance around" that regulation, so to speak. Big corporate shows called "industrials" were popular in Chicago, and from time to time, casting directors would observe classes and hire dancers for them. Frequently I was chosen, and I was eventually able to branch out and book other work outside of the studio that didn't conflict with my class schedule.

A big advantage of being attached to a studio in a new city is that many jobs are posted on the bulletin board, and other performers talk about other jobs that aren't posted. The "word of mouth" gigs were more immediate, and you often had to know someone or be invited to get into those auditions.

Being black made snagging those jobs even tougher. There was usually only one spot open for a black dancer, and someone who had already worked for the company normally took it. That made it especially tough for someone new to break in. I bonded with Anthony Hollins, another black dancer on scholarship, who was nearly as motivated as I was. We put our heads together and decided that since we had both done a good number of high-profile industrials, we had what it took to form our own production company. We did this while we were still on scholarship. Can you say *ambitious*?

To avoid competition with the major production companies, we catered to a niche market of nightclubs. Dance fashion shows were a big deal in Chicago at that time, especially at some of the trendy clubs, and we made them our specialty. Clubs and clients liked using attractive model types who could dance and bring the fashions to life in a way that was active, fun, and athletic. We used some of the dancers from the studio and auditioned others in the city. We registered with the Chicago Convention and Tourism Bureau. To protect our scholarships, our rehearsals were in the early evenings after classes, and our performances were almost always on the weekends.

About six months after I started at Giordano's, I heard that a production of *The Wiz*, the famed black musical adaptation of *The Wizard of Oz*, was to be produced at the Lincolnshire Marriot, a respected Actors' Equity theater tied to a suburban resort. In this particular production, the cast would be racially mixed with a white Dorothy, a white Tin Man, and a racially diverse ensemble.

I was enjoying studying dance, but of course I missed singing. For our winter dance concert at Giordano's, there was a gap in the program that needed to be filled so someone could make a costume change. I volunteered to sing a Christmas song a cappella to cover it. The director was skeptical because she had never heard me sing, so I broke into "O Holy Night." The class gasped and cheered. The evening of the actual performance, I got thunderous applause after the song. The next day, the director congratulated me and gave me a very curious look as if to say, "Remember the rule about not auditioning." She didn't say it, but I could feel it. She could probably sense that I was getting restless. She might also have been picking up on a bit of guilt.

The Lincolnshire Marriott is about an hour outside of Chicago. I was non-Equity but had heard that if you showed up for an Equity call, you might have a chance to audition at the end if there was time. I drove all the way out there with my sheet music, dance clothes, and crossed fingers. I was the last dancer allowed to audition and was blessed with a callback a few days later.

I will never forget the call I got from the Marriott saying that I had booked my first Equity show after only six months in Chicago. I had to have yet another difficult conversation, this time with Gus's daughter, Nan Giordano, the director of the studio, to confess that I'd booked the show. I confided that as much as I loved dance, musical theater was my true love. I assured her that it was not my intention to leave the program, and that I would continue to take as many classes as I could and fulfill my duties as a scholarship recipient.

The Wiz was something that I needed to do both artistically and financially, although I didn't tell Nan that I flat-out needed the money. Most of the students on scholarship were being supported by their families and could fully focus on their training. As much as my family loved and supported me, there just wasn't any money to spare.

My experience with *The Wiz* was phenomenal! The color-blind casting of the show got Actors' Equity all up in arms and even made the national news. People had strong opinions about a racially mixed version of *The Wiz*, which had been specifically created as an all-black musical, and the controversy made it a hot ticket in town. I was cast in the show as a dancer and understudied the role of the Scarecrow, but never got a chance to perform it. I was simply happy to be working in my first show with professional union actors, and I soaked up as much of their experience as possible. It was through many of their firsthand examples that I witnessed the importance of establishing good working relationships, maintaining professionalism, and upholding an excellent and reliable reputation. I knew to show up on time, not pretend to know what I didn't know, and keep my eyes and ears open to learn as much as I could from the seasoned professionals around me.

After the show closed, I went back to full-time studies at Giordano's studio. It was challenging coming back down to earth after such an amazing high. I put my focus back on training, auditioning, and booking industrials, but I missed the family atmosphere that goes into doing an actual musical. Several months later, another dream came true when the Lincolnshire Marriott called and offered me a job as a dancer in their production of *Evita*. A dancer who had worked there often had asked to be released from his contract to take advantage of another opportunity. I was told that because of my discipline, professionalism, and likability during *The Wiz*, the creative team thought of me and offered me the job without an audition.

Now, I had learned that once you joined the actors' union and "become Equity," you could no longer do non-Equity theater (except in specific, limited circumstances set forth by the union). Since *The Wiz* had been my first union show, I hadn't been obligated to join. Not knowing when I would book another Equity show, I had held off on joining (and paying the dues required). After being cast in *Evita* without an audition, my instincts told me that it was time to take another leap of faith and join the union. Booking *Evita* was a sign to me that it was time to be a professional musical theater performer. I finished my year on scholarship at the studio and did not look back.

LIFE CAN BE A *DREAMGIRLS* TOUR

Soon after *Evita*, I made my Equity debut in a principal role at the Lincolnshire Marriott. I was double-cast as both Johnny Casino and Teen Angel in *Grease*.

My next big Chicago job was at the Candlelight Dinner Playhouse, one of the first regional theaters to produce *Dreamgirls*. Being cast in the coveted role of Curtis Taylor Jr. took me back to a wonderful memory from my senior year of high school at SCPA. I had run into Jack Louiso, the artistic director of Performing Arts, in the hallway right after spring break. He was full of energy because he had spent his break in New York City and had seen a handful of Broadway shows. He pulled me aside and told me that he had seen one show in particular that was revolutionizing Broadway, and that there was a part in it that I would someday play—Curtis Taylor Jr.

I went to the record store that day after school and purchased the soundtrack. *Dreamgirls* has the distinction of being the first album that I ever bought. The entire score was amazing, but nothing moved me more than hearing Ben Harney—who won the Tony Award for best actor in a musical that year for playing the role of Curtis Taylor Jr.—sing "When I First Saw You." It was one of the most beautiful, warm tones that I'd ever heard in a man's voice. I became obsessed and ached to play that role.

I didn't have an agent at the time, so when I got the phenomenal call offering me the part, I gladly accepted and asked them if I could call them back, since I knew that I would have to negotiate the contract myself. I had no idea how much a principal in a role in a big new show should be making or what kinds of perks to ask for. I was ecstatic to have been offered my dream role and, like most performers who love their work, would have done it for free. But in the business of show business, free was not an option. With no agent to represent me, I knew the importance of making a good, professional first impression with the producers. I wanted to sound confident when I called them back to discuss my contract, and I needed to use a tone that conveyed humility, but also one that suggested that I knew what I was worth.

One of the most important lessons I have learned is to not be afraid to ask for help. I reached out to some of my friends who were already playing major principal roles and whose advice and character I respected. I made a list of things to ask for. They informed me that I would not get everything on my list but that I should ask anyway and settle someplace in the middle. I was anxious, but I gathered my nerves, returned the call to the Candlelight, and negotiated as calmly and confidently as I could. The final contract wasn't going to make me rich, but I was content because it was more money than I had ever made before.

Dreamgirls was a huge success. Some theatrical producers who were looking for a touring company came to our production and offered it to our group. At the age of twenty-four, I took off on my first national tour, traveling the country as the male lead in my favorite musical and having the time of my life.

Some of the cast had been brought in from a West Coast *Dreamgirls* to replace Chicago actors who had opted not to travel. Others had performed in the Broadway company or tours of the show. I reveled in every story they told about their experiences. Our tour was categorized as "an Experimental Bus and Truck" tour. This meant that we traveled from city to city in

"Greyhound-like buses" and flew only if absolutely necessary.

Whatever the *method* of travel, there was a lot of packing and unpacking. Most of our tour consisted of split weeks, which meant we'd spend a couple of days in one city performing, load up on the bus immediately after the final show, and then drive through the night to the next city where we were scheduled to perform. It was a rough schedule, and I definitely paid my dues. They don't call Broadway musical performers gypsies for nothing. Have skills, will travel!

Dreamgirls had made its Broadway debut in 1981. The first tour had been in 1983, and there had already been a second, so our production was considered a third- or fourth-tier tour. Some of the Broadway and first-tour veterans grumbled about many of the uncomfortable conditions that were part of our life as a company, but this was my first tour, and I was in heaven. I was performing, seeing the country, and making more money than I'd ever made in my entire life. Sure, the daily grind was sometimes rough, but the hard work and difficult conditions on the road were all part of the training, and I believe to this day that all the experiences, exhilarating or exhausting, were worth it.

One of the highlights of the tour was our gig in Las Vegas, which played right into my childhood fantasies of being a casino headliner like Sammy Davis Jr., Frank Sinatra, or Johnny Mathis. We performed there at the famed Aladdin Casino (now Planet Hollywood Resort & Casino). It was a big deal at that time for a touring show to be booked in a casino, because Broadway shows run longer than the time slots allotted for shows in Vegas. So, for our weeklong run there, *Dreamgirls* was cut in half.

One of my favorite memories is the night that most of the cast got tickets to see Ann-Margret perform at the renowned Caesars Palace. Like Diana Ross, Lola Falana, and Cher, Ann-Margret epitomized the glamour of Vegas in the 1980s. We had less than forty-five minutes to finish our show, get changed, and head further up the Strip. We literally ran up the street as a group and got to Caesars Palace just in time for the performance. Her show was everything that I had dreamed a big Vegas show would be. It was glitzy, sexy, and dazzling, and she was absolutely stunning! After the show, Ann-Margret invited us back to her dressing room for a meet and greet. Completely starstruck, I just stood there without saying a word while she autographed my souvenir program.

I needed an agent to negotiate the *Dreamgirls* tour contract, because I was way out of my depth. I had become close to Lynette DuPree, who played Effie in the show, and her New York–based agent negotiated my tour contract as a favor to her. I didn't actually get to meet him until we played New Haven, Connecticut, the closest our tour got to New York City.

That was another highlight of the tour for me since we played at the famed Shubert Theatre in New Haven, which is legendary as the theater where hit shows traditionally played out of town before heading to Broadway in New York. And I now felt like I was a part of that history.

After seeing me in the show, Lynette's agent told me that he thought I had great potential and offered to represent me if I ever moved to New York. I told him that while I was on tour, Chicago was still my home, but also said that I would love to move to New York—though I wanted to arrive with a job in hand. I assured him that if he submitted me for projects we both agreed were worth it, I would travel to New York to audition. I still didn't have an agent in Chicago, but just like that, I had one in New York City.

On our day off in New Haven, Lynette and I took the quick seventy-five-mile train ride down to the Big Apple to explore. I'll never forget using a pay phone to call my mother and tell her that I was calling from the heart of Times Square, the center of the world!

The number one highlight of the entire tour, however, was playing in my hometown at Cincinnati's Taft Theatre. No words can fully describe how wonderful it is to go home as a lead in a show that you love. We played Cincinnati for a week, and every time I came out of the stage door, family and friends from every part of my life were waiting for me. Former teachers and classmates all made it a point to let me know how proud of me they were, and the local news did a wonderful segment about my triumphant return.

Lynette and I were the only two cast members who never missed a performance. But, unfortunately, I had to leave *Dreamgirls* about a month before the tour closed. I developed a hernia on my right side. I had ignored it and continued to dance through the pain for as long as I could. As much as I hated to say goodbye, I knew that I needed to have it repaired if I wanted a career beyond *Dreamgirls*. The laser surgery was expedient, but the recovery process was no joke. I was led to believe that I would have the surgery, spend a short time in light pain recuperating, and then walk out of the hospital. The advertisements made it sound so simple. Hah! I was totally blindsided. I was bedridden for almost two weeks, during which time I really got to experience first-hand how all the different body parts connect!

FURTHER TALES OF THE WINDY CITY

After I got back on my feet, I auditioned for industrials, but things had slowed down quite a bit while I'd been away. I was also starting to feel that familiar restlessness. I'd saved a decent amount of money while on tour, but that money would only last me for so long. I collected unemployment because I was qualified, but I didn't like the feeling of being inactive even if I was collecting a check.

I reached a point where there was nothing happening in theater or commercial work, so I applied for another fantasy job as a waiter. I know it sounds crazy, but I'd always been curious about waiting tables. My friends considered me a good host. I loved seeing people happy and comfortable, and I liked the fact that it was fast-moving and seemed like it could be fun.

Waiting tables at Bennigan's restaurant, right across Michigan Avenue from the Art Institute of Chicago, was fun at first, but of course I missed performing. My Chicago theater dreams had come true—going from the chorus to lead roles—and I was starting to feel like it might be time to move on. But I didn't know when or how.

Just when waiting tables stopped being fun, I got another miracle call from the Lincolnshire Marriott with an invitation to join the ensemble for *South Pacific*. It was a difficult call for me because, as much as I missed theater, I didn't want to go back to the ensemble after working as a lead. As I was mulling over my decision, things went downhill at the restaurant almost immediately. The same day that I'd received the offer and at the end of a winter shift, one of my coworkers walked out with my jacket, and I don't mean by accident. The jacket held my wallet, keys, and that evening's tips. I called a friend who had an emergency set of keys, and he came and picked me up since I had no coat in the dead of winter. I discussed my dilemma with him and decided that, although I was uncertain, the robbery was a sign that I should take the ensemble job.

A few weeks later, there was a string of additional unfortunate incidents. I was already stressed about my financial situation and when and how I was going to make my next move. So, I went to the gym early one morning to make myself feel better. My plan was to get some positive exercise, treat myself to a grand breakfast, and then drop off my rent to my landlord, which always made me feel responsible. Feeling invigorated after my workout, I went back to the locker room only to discover that someone had broken into my locker and stolen my wallet, which had all the cash for my rent. I was devastated and had to replace everything yet again.

The real blow, however, came when my car broke down just before rehearsals for *South Pacific*. Between the robberies and the cost of making my car operable again, I was left feeling emotionally and financially overwhelmed. I didn't know if I'd even have enough money to make it to rehearsals for the show. I had no choice but to do the one thing that I dreaded ever having to do: borrow money. I called home, and my family put together as much as they could. Friends chipped in too, but it still wasn't enough.

A couple of my good friends recommended that I call the Actors Fund. I had never heard of it, but they were certain that the fund could help me. I called the next morning and spoke to someone at the Chicago branch.

When I told them of my misfortune, they asked me to fax over my rent and utility receipts, and within a few days, I got a check to cover them. I was beyond relieved and was able to use the money I had borrowed to hold me over until my first *South Pacific* paycheck.

Most actors lived on the North Side of town, but by this time I had moved to the South Side, where the apartments were bigger. The Marriott in Lincolnshire, Illinois, was now no less than a ninety-minute drive from my apartment. When my car broke down, I had to take a bus and two trains just to catch a ride with one of my North Side castmates and then drive with them another hour just to get to rehearsals. Then I had to do the reverse to get home at night. It was stressful and tiring, but I did my very best to focus on the positives—like the fact that I had a job.

For *South Pacific*, the creative team hired a black New York actress named Tina Fabrique to play Bloody Mary. We were the only two black cast members and we bonded immediately. I showed her around the city a bit and introduced her to some of my friends to help make her comfortable, and she was kind enough to let me pick her brain and ask her a million questions about life as a black actor in New York City.

It was during the run of *South Pacific* that I received a life-changing call from my agent in New York. Since I'd left the *Dreamgirls* tour, I'd made two trips to New York for off-Broadway auditions that he'd arranged for me.

I didn't have much money, so I took the least expensive mode of transportation I could find. On my first trip, I took a Greyhound bus that happened to stop in Cleveland, where my sister Anna lived. She met me at the station to see me and bring me a meal. We lost track of time, however, and I missed the bus, which had all my belongings on it. By the time I got the next bus to New York City and checked Greyhound's lost and found, my things had disappeared, leaving me to audition in the clothes I had been wearing for twenty-four hours. Thankfully, I had my wallet on me.

On my second trip, I took a train ride that made a thousand stops along the way—and my belongings were stolen while I slept! Not to sound overly dramatic, but I was feeling like Job! I had always believed the adage that the universe never challenged you with more than you could handle, but I was at this point thinking that the universe had made a big mistake with me in assuming that I was a lot stronger than I actually was. I hoped and prayed that all the consecutive setbacks were somehow preparing me for something better.

As it turns out, my agent was calling about a new show out of London called *Miss Saigon*. He said that the audition slots were coveted but that he had been able to get me one. Thankfully, my audition slot was for late on a Monday afternoon, because I was off on Monday and Tuesday. I had just paid back my loans and landed back in the black financially, so I was reluctant to do it, but I had no choice but to splurge for a plane ticket. It was the only way to get there and back without missing any performances of *South Pacific*. I told myself that whether or not the audition resulted in a job, I needed to fully invest in it, to be engaged in the experience, and to learn whatever I could from it. That's something I try to do in every aspect of my life. If you focus on results, you can miss both the lessons and the rewards of the process.

I had less than a week to prepare before for my first big Broadway audition, and I immediately absorbed myself in everything I could find about the show and the history of the war in Vietnam. I purchased the original London cast album and listened to it on repeat. I could tell from the pictures in the CD case that the character of John was white in the show, but his song, "Bui Doi," resonated deeply with me. "Bui Doi" is an emotional, vocally challenging song that fit well in my range, and I really wanted to sing it. I thought it might be a bold choice to go into my audition with this song knowing that the character was conceived as being Caucasian, but you only get one chance to make a first impression and I wanted mine to be a good one.

I reached out to some of my more experienced colleagues for advice about auditioning. I told them that I felt moved and inspired to sing "Bui Doi." They warned me that sometimes the creative team doesn't like to hear songs from the show because they get tired of hearing the same music over and over all day. I was a little dismayed, but my instincts told me that if I sang this heartbreaking song at my audition, I had a good shot at being cast as one of the soldiers in the show.

I studied "Bui Doi" at first as a monologue to more truthfully tell the story, and then as a song to communicate it convincingly. In case I wouldn't be permitted to sing it, I rehearsed a back-up song. It was an anthem with a similar powerful message: "You'll Never Walk Alone" from *Carousel*.

Gratefully, my first Broadway audition was not in a studio. Just as I'd always fantasized, it was on the stage of a Broadway theater, the Golden Theatre on Forty-Fifth Street right off Times Square. My name was called, I walked out onto the stage, and a voice from somewhere in the back of the dark theater asked me what I would like to sing. I answered with sort of a question in my voice: "I would like to sing 'Bui Doi,'" literally crossing my fingers behind my back. There was a pause and then light whispers among the creative team. And then the voice said, "Okay." I felt instant relief that I would be able to see my vision through and sing that glorious song for them. I took a deep breath and then performed the song as if I were the character delivering his message to the entire theater. I was far less nervous than I was excited, largely because of all the thorough preparation I had done before.

I wore my best suit to my audition, because I'd discovered in my research that the character wears a suit at this point in the show—he's addressing the song's message to a large group at a conference. I was auditioning for the ensemble, but I wanted to commit as fully as I could to the character, the song, and the setting and maybe be considered as an understudy for the role.

Being in a big theater with light on the stage and darkness out in the house felt magical. I wanted to make a memorable impression. I knew that the team of people somewhere out there in the dark would be casting other shows in the future, and I wanted to be remembered. In addition, I wanted my investment in the hours of rehearsal and research to pay off.

After I finished the song, the voice in the dark said to me that they were aware that I had planned to fly back to Chicago that evening after my audition. He asked if I would consider delaying my flight until the next day so that I could come back for the dance call later that evening. I said yes before he finished asking me.

I had about four hours to kill before the dance call. First, I found the nearest phone and called the airline to change my flight, excited about my callback and thrilled that I'd get an unexpected overnight stay in the Big Apple. Next I called one of my New York buddies, Brian Chandler, to tell him the great news and ask if I could sleep on his couch—and also for an additional favor. I offered to treat him to lunch and dinner as a "thank you" in exchange for about an hour of his time. I needed to find an army-surplus store and see what kind of military-style clothing I could find for my dance call. After lunch, he took me to Kaufman's Army & Navy surplus store on Forty-Second Street.

I found a pair of camouflage track shorts, a green army cap, and a camouflage muscle shirt, and I topped it all off by splurging on some black combat boots that zipped up the side. They had cushioned rubber soles, so I felt comfortable dancing in them. I wanted to look like a physically fit soldier in training and for my new dance ensemble to fit well, but not be too tight or distracting. I tried on the outfit for Brian to get his opinion and he gave me the thumbs-up that I looked like a GI.

I got back to the Golden Theatre about forty-five minutes before the call to change and stretch on the stage with the other guys. There was one other guy who was dressed military style for the callback. He came over and introduced himself as Henry Menendez. We complimented each other on our committed period outfits and then shook hands. As we stretched and chatted, Henry filled me in on some of the latest *Miss Saigon* gossip. He told me that his first audition for the show had been over a year ago and that this was his fourth or fifth time being seen, but only his first dance call. I had already heard the rumors about the show's possible delay or even cancellation. It was all over the news, and the controversy was driving up the show's advance sales. Because of the racial sensitivities regarding the

171

show and the threatened boycotting, no one was sure when the show would actually be cast or if it would happen at all.

Similar to the controversy surrounding *The Wiz* years earlier in Chicago (but multiplied by a thousand), *Miss Saigon* was the subject of intense racial protests. A lot of it had to do with the casting of Jonathan Pryce, a white English actor who had won great praise for his performance in the original London cast in the principal role of the Engineer, a mixed-race character with a Vietnamese name. The controversy and publicity surrounding a show that was already highly anticipated made *Miss Saigon* a hot ticket on Broadway even before rehearsals started. Clearly, race and casting were frontier issues that were being explored and debated with sometimes-imperfect results.

Listening to Henry share his story on his lengthy journey through previous auditions just for this show left me feeling a little discouraged, so I set my focus on stretching and being as present in the moment as I could. I was also mentally preparing myself to retain and follow whatever combinations were about to be thrown my way.

The choreographer, Bob Avian (the legendary Michael Bennett's collaborator for many years), soon called us all to attention. Henry and I wished each other luck, and the dance call commenced. We were all taught a great military-style combination that required strength and precision, and my chosen audition ensemble made me feel confident—and like I was really in military training. Both Henry and I made it down to the final group of guys.

After the callback, we congratulated each other on making it that far and hoped that we would see each other again at rehearsals if and when the show happened, and if we were both blessed to be cast.

It turned out to be a jam-packed few days. I had flown into New York's LaGuardia Airport as scheduled Monday morning, auditioned that afternoon, and had the additional dance call that evening. I spent Tuesday in Manhattan catching up with friends in the city, and then, on Wednesday, flew back to Chicago early enough to make my matinee of *South Pacific*.

When I got back, I was very doubtful that I would hear any news for quite a while, yet still exhilarated by the entire experience.

Two nights later, at around 12:30 A.M. Chicago time, I got a call from the late, great casting director Vinnie Liff. Vinnie asked me if I was ready to move to New York and make my Broadway debut in the ensemble of *Miss Saigon*. I jumped up and down, yelling and screaming like a kid on Christmas morning. Vinnie congratulated me on a great audition and told me that two-time Tony Award winner Hinton Battle had been cast as John Thomas, and that I would be one of his three understudies.

John was being cast as a black man for the Broadway

production. This was even greater news to me because I had trusted my instincts and sung the song that resonated with me regardless of the character's race. It was through this entire experience that I realized how much details matter. I was on the phone into the wee hours of the morning, calling everyone I knew to share my good news. I was light-headed with joy! Being cast in my first Broadway show after my first Broadway audition while still living in Chicago might not have officially qualified as a miracle, but it felt like one.

Before I left Chicago, a group of friends threw me a big going-away party. There were many people there from the theater community that I did not know. It started off as a celebration, but the tone started to change when some Chicago actors took issue with the *Miss Saigon* casting. One of them approached me and asked me if I was really going to take the job. I didn't know what to say. Of course I was thrilled to have the opportunity to move to New York and make my debut in a show that had not only been a hit in London but that confronted significant real-world problems. I couldn't figure out why he would ask me such a confrontational question at a party that was being thrown for me.

Other pessimists at the party warned me about the dangers of New York and told me that I should be careful and watch my back—and basically be on guard and afraid. What started as a celebration turned into a serious downer. A mentor of mine at the time pulled me over to the side and asked me what was wrong. I tried to put him off, but he could see that my energy had shifted. I told him about some of the negative conversations I was having. Initially, I had been so excited about this opportunity. But now I was feeling like I should be worried.

He then gave me some great advice. "Alton," he said, "don't ever accept other people's projections. The negative things that they mentioned will probably never happen to you. You are excited to go to New York. You are ready and open for the experience. You are expecting it to be fantastic, and so, for you, it will be."

I breathed a huge sigh of relief. He understood what I was feeling. I managed to ignore the negative input that I'd gotten at the party and accept that it was totally fine for me to be excited about the experiences I was about to have. I realized that the universe had been closing doors for me in Chicago so that I could stop looking behind me and move *forward* toward my new set of wonderful adventures. The next day I sent the last of my boxes to New York City, and a few days after that, January 25, 1991, I jumped on a plane to begin my new life in the Big Apple.

Every spiritual program I have ever encountered recommends staying in the now, keeping your head in the present, not getting bogged down in the past or scattered in hypothetical futures. And it is thoroughly good advice, up to a point. Being centered in the now keeps our eye on the work at hand. It means applying all the personal, professional, and emotional tools at our disposal to making every day the best day it can be. But sometimes the present does not seem to be enough. Or it feels downright hideous. Part of living in the present is acknowledging that every day is a single step on a long journey, sometimes knowable, and sometimes way outside our power to understand. Both good and bad days will pass away into something new and ever changing.

It's a challenge to stay in the present when the present is not fulfilling. You may feel that you need to do what's in your power to change things. This is sometimes frightening and sometimes liberating. It can be a combination of both. You may want to go to Hawaii, but sitting in Atlanta waiting to be teleported probably won't get you there. You probably need to save some money, pick an appropriate date, and make a plane reservation. Your instincts help identify what to do: stay or go. But your intellect and your instincts can work together to make decisions and to take actions.

It is always good to remember that it's often dark-est before the dawn and that what might at times feel like punishment may actually be a sign that something better and more suited to you is just beyond the hori-zon. Sometimes the change will be the result of your hard work, patience, and perseverance. Sometimes it will seem to come as a bolt out of the blue, beyond your power or control. Living in the now also means having a sane and realistic look at ourselves. Keeping the ego in balance is a trick, but it gets easier with experience.

And finally, when the break comes, there is nothing more rewarding than having overcome your doubts and investing energy into the preparation and creation of healthy mental space to walk confidently into a won-derful new opportunity.

FOOD FOR THOUGHT

1. Can you honestly say you've taken a big risk in order to create the life you envisioned for yourself? If so, how did it work out? If not, what held you back, and what were the consequences?

2. In work and personal situations, do you give yourself proper credit for your assets? Are you honest about your weak spots, and are you willing to work on them?

3. Have you ever been hired below the level of your talents and capabilities, as almost everybody has at one time or another? Did you resent being overqualified and allow that resentment to be seen and affect your work, or did you give your assigned task all your energy and creativity?

4. Do you maintain the attitude that you can learn from any experience?

5. How do we know when it's time to move on, and what is the best way to handle letting go of the present to move into the future? Can a step backward on the career path actually be a leap forward?

6. What are the ways you can "invest in yourself" that are not just financial?

Faith is taking the first step even when you don't see the whole staircase.

—Martin Luther King Jr.

Chapter 10

MY FIRST BITE
OF THE BIG APPLE

Charting new territory can be frightening, but there is nothing like the excitement of a new beginning. When you are blazing a trail, it can be difficult to not let others— especially loved ones—discourage you or project their fears and concerns onto you. You are not obligated to justify your dreams, adjust them, or shrink them for anyone else. Your responsibility to yourself is to sustain the tenacity you may need to manifest your dreams.

My friend Brian Chandler, who was extremely helpful to me when I came to the city for my *Miss Saigon* audition, offered to let me sublet his apartment in Hell's Kitchen, the Manhattan neighborhood due west of the Theater District. He would be away doing a play, leaving me two months to get settled and find a place of my own. I arrived at the apartment in the early evening to drop off my bags. I was exhausted, but Rufus Bonds, my old friend from the Conservatory of Music, who lived in the same building, tempted me with a play he wanted me to see. So off we went to the Ethel Barrymore Theatre to see *Mule Bone* by Zora Neale Hurston and Langston Hughes, two of the leading lights of the Harlem Renaissance. It was my first theatergoing experience as a New Yorker, and my first as a member of the Broadway community.

The next day Rufus took me to the Galaxy Diner on Ninth Avenue and Forty-Sixth Street, a well-known Broadway hangout. It was a Saturday morning and the place was already buzzing with theatergoers and actors preparing for matinee performances. On our way to the register to pay the bill, I noticed someone I thought I recognized having a meal with his family. It was Ben Harney, the original, Tony-winning Curtis from *Dreamgirls*! I almost jumped out of my skin! I grabbed Rufus excitedly and told him that one of my musical theater heroes was sitting in this very diner. He laughed, told me to calm down, and then took me over to meet him. Meeting one of my idols at the beginning of my first full day in New York City was another sign that I was exactly where I was supposed to be.

The night before the first rehearsal of *Miss Saigon* felt like the night before the first day of school. I could barely sleep I was so excited. I catnapped more than slept and had vivid dreams of getting lost in the subway and being late for the first rehearsal. Rufus assured me that the trip to 890 Broadway was a snap, and thousands of actors, singers, and dancers had made it before, since the old building, once owned by Michael Bennett, the director and choreographer of *A Chorus Line*, was famous for its rehearsal halls. I woke up far earlier than I needed and made it to rehearsal with plenty of time to spare.

The first day was a breakfast meet and greet. I remember walking into a huge room already full of people and an enormous buffet. The first person I recognized was two-time Tony Award winner Hinton Battle, who was cast in the principal role of John Thomas. I'd been a huge fan for years and had seen him perform on TV dozens of times. He was another one of my black musical theater heroes. I was immediately starstruck. The second person I noticed was Vinnie Liff, the casting director. Vinnie came over and shook my hand to congratulate and welcome me. I told him that I was thrilled to be there, and beyond excited that Hinton Battle was in the room and that I would actually be working with him.

It was Vinnie who then took me over to Hinton and introduced us. As I was shaking his hand, I turned into a blabbering, geeky fan telling him how much and for how long I'd loved his work. He was very kind and said that he was looking forward to working with me as well.

Being cast in a Broadway show is like making it into the NBA. But being cast in *Miss Saigon* was especially coveted. Everyone in the cast was aware that the show was already a financial success based on preopening sales, and that we were the chosen few who were blessed to be a part of it. To be in *Miss Saigon* at that place—and in that time—was a very big deal.

One day in rehearsal, the choreographer, Bob Avian, asked me to stay behind and work with him during a lunch break. I was already a fan of Bob's and knew he had been Michael Bennett's cochoreographer on *A Chorus Line,* which originally ran on Broadway from 1975 to 1990. Toward the end of the session, he told me that he'd been watching me and noticed how quickly I'd picked up the choreography. He wanted to offer me the position of company dance captain but had found out that I was slated to be Hinton Battle's first cover for the role of John. That was news to me—and thrilling news at that! But I couldn't do both. As flattered as I was to be offered dance captain, the possibility of performing a lead role on Broadway was too much to pass up.

I picked understudy, and the rehearsal period commenced. About five or six weeks later, we moved from the rehearsal hall to the Broadway Theatre, one of the few "Broadway" theaters that is actually *on* Broadway.

Soon thereafter, the "Sitzprobe" was scheduled. Taken from the German word *Sitzprobe*, meaning "seated rehearsal" (but pronounced with just two syllables in English), the Sitzprobe is always exciting. It's the first time the performers sing through the entire score with the orchestra (instead of a single rehearsal piano). As a rule, a Sitzprobe is a closed rehearsal, held in a music studio, but because of all the media attention surrounding *Miss Saigon*, our Sitzprobe was held at the famed Hammerstein Ballroom, which was built in 1906 by the great impresario Oscar Hammerstein (father of the famous Broadway composer) as a rival venue to the Metropolitan Opera right down the street. The hype surrounding the opening of *Miss Saigon* had reached such a high level that every arm of the press was on hand.

The anticipation was electric, and everyone was ready to begin—cast, company, orchestra, producers, press. But one person had not yet arrived: Hinton Battle, who was probably stuck in a taxi. Given the pressure to begin, the musical director asked if any of Hinton's understudies knew his part. At first none of us reacted. We hadn't yet started understudy rehearsals. I knew the part but was embarrassed to admit it. Finally, I spoke up and said, "Yes, I know it." He then said, "Great, we can begin."

When the orchestra hit those first few notes, the place went crazy. After only hearing the piano version of the show for the past month and half, we were amazed at the different instruments that accompanied the melodies. I only got through a couple of Hinton's lines before he showed up to thunderous applause. He jumped in without missing a beat and the rest of the Sitzprobe went off without a hitch.

The show opened to rave reviews on April 11, 1991, one day after my twenty-sixth birthday. The opening night party was a night that I will never forget. My date for the event was my number one fan: Marietta White, my mother. At the party, a gala the likes of which I'd never seen, my mother told me with tears flowing down her face how proud she was of me, her baby boy, for being so courageous and disciplined and working so hard to make this dream come true. Her words were the most important and memorable part of that magnificent evening.

MY FIRST STARRING ROLE ON BROADWAY!

Miss Saigon won three Tony Awards, all for acting: Best Actor in a Musical for Jonathan Pryce, Best Actress for Lea Salonga, and Best Featured Actor for Hinton Battle. Just a few weeks after the awards show, I went on for Battle as John for the first time. I can happily report that family was in attendance! Two of my sisters, Paula and Darlene, had come to town for their first New York visit and were already scheduled to see the evening show. That afternoon I got the call that Hinton would be out that night. I had injured my wrist a few days before, and stage management was worried that I couldn't perform. The helicopter evacuation scene in *Miss Saigon* is very physical, and they did not want me to reinjure myself. I assured them that I would be fine. (There was no way I wasn't going on!)

I wrapped my injury and then attended the mandatory "fight call," a safety measure, before the show. Then, with supportive cheers from my fellow cast members, I went on to make my debut as a principal on Broadway. Having family there to witness it was more than I could have asked for.

But it got even better. One day after an understudy rehearsal, Mitchell Lemsky, the associate director, pulled me aside to congratulate me. I thanked him but wasn't sure what he was congratulating me for. He then informed me that I would be performing the role of John twice a week and seemed surprised that I didn't know. Performing a role, even two times a week, is a step beyond standing by as a cover.

Apparently, after the Tonys, Hinton had renegotiated his contract to perform six times a week instead of eight. It seemed a bit odd not to be hearing this great news from my new agents at J. Michael Bloom & Associates (a foreshadowing of things to come), but I was elated. I couldn't believe it! Less than a year after moving to New York, I was appearing in a big old fat Broadway hit, and now I would be performing a lead role regularly twice a week! And not just any role, but one that included the unforgettable, heart-wrenching "Bui Doi," a song about the abandoned interracial children of American soldiers and Vietnamese women, one of the most poignant sequences in the show.

Toward the end of the first year of the show, the producers extended an offer to me to take over the role of John Thomas on a full-time basis. Hinton, being the great role model that he is, not only coached me but offered advice on what I should ask for during my negotiations. When I approached my agents with some of my concerns, they told me that there were no negotiations to be done and that there was already a set dollar amount in place for the role. I was disappointed because they hadn't seemed to even try to negotiate anything for me or care to hear what I might have liked. This left me feeling doubtful about them and their representation of me, but I shifted my focus to the work and my gratitude for this new opportunity.

It was also around this time that I began to look for an acting teacher to help me stay fresh and hopefully help me branch out into TV and film work. Hinton introduced me to Alan Savage, the teacher he'd studied with to prepare for the role of John. Alan taught his acting class out of the living room of his East Side home. You didn't have to audition, but you did have to be recommended by a present student to be accepted. Alan's technique was all about listening and reacting. I loved that his method worked for any kind of performing, whether it was for film and TV, theater, or simply delivering the lyrics of a song truthfully.

After taking on the role of John full-time, I started thinking ahead about how to make the most of the opportunity and visibility I was being given. I decided to make another dream come true and do my first nightclub act. Cabaret appeals to me because it is the perfect opportunity to be yourself, as opposed to playing a role. Many performers are terrified when it comes to doing their own club act, because exposing yourself that way makes you incredibly vulnerable. But I think every performer should do it at least once, because there is nothing like the validation that you get from intimately performing material that you are fully connected to.

I made my New York City cabaret debut in 1992 at Don't Tell Mama on Restaurant Row (West Forty-Sixth Street between Eighth and Ninth Avenues). I performed it as a benefit with all the proceeds going to the Actors Fund out of gratitude for their help when I had been in such dire need in Chicago just a few years before.

After playing the role of John for a year, something unpleasant and absolutely unexpected happened. Without a hint of a warning, I was told that the company would not be renewing my contract. I wasn't given an explanation as to why. Even though I knew it wasn't personal, it felt that way, and it hurt my feelings deeply. On the evening of my last performance, Mitchell Lemsky, the associate director, presented me with flowers and a bottle of Dom Perignon on behalf of the production. I tried to be gracious and act as if I weren't affected by it being my last show. He congratulated me on doing a great job and said that he hoped that I would come back to the show at some point.

I'm not proud of it, but I let my pride and ego get the better of me and said, "Thank you, but no thank you."

I put on a brave face and told him that I appreciated the offer but that I was very much looking forward to moving forward. I was speaking from insecurity, immaturity, and disappointment. It felt easier to seem strong and "over it" than to show how hurt I was for not being asked back. I loved playing John and wondered what I might have done for them to not want me to continue. Truthfully, I was also afraid that *Miss Saigon* might be my first and only Broadway experience.

To counter my disappointment, instead of having a typical closing-night gathering, I performed another benefit cabaret for the Actors Fund at Eighty-Eights (a Greenwich Village piano bar, since closed, that had a luxurious second-floor cabaret space). The performance was scheduled immediately after my last show and had food catered for my guests.

Although planning the benefit was a healthy, productive way to channel my hurt feelings, I learned a lot from my final exchange with the associate director about relationships and the consequence of taking things personally. I am grateful that I had the awareness that I was burning a major bridge and used it as incentive to work hard, succeed, and not need to go back to *Miss Saigon*. Most importantly, I learned that how you exit a situation is just as important as how you enter one—if not more so.

Fortunately, about two months before my contract ended with *Miss Saigon*, I was offered a part in another life-changing role, not on Broadway, but back at the

Marriott Theatre in Lincolnshire. The role was that of Jackie Robinson in a musical called *The First*.

I wasn't a huge sports fan, but I definitely knew who Jackie Robinson was and what he represented in terms of integrating the game of baseball: when Jackie Robinson first appeared with the Brooklyn Dodgers on April 15, 1947, he broke a color barrier that had been in effect in Major League Baseball since the 1880s. What I didn't know until I did research on him for the role was that he was UCLA's first four-letter man, the first to excel in four major sports at one school. I also found out that he faced much adversity in his young life and that it had prepared him to be the exceptional human being that he became.

Robinson's mother had moved the family from the southern United States to California and into an all-white neighborhood, thereby integrating it. Jackie had become accustomed to being called names at school, withstanding and excelling in spite of incredible pressure. He was the perfect black man to go out onto the baseball field, ignore the insults being hurled at him during the game, and thrive.

This was a huge revelation for me. I identified with his having to deal with and persevere through verbal abuse even as a kid. It gave me hope that, as nervous as I was about leaving *Miss Saigon*, there might be more wonderful experiences waiting for me. Jackie Robinson's story also taught me that it takes a combination of things to make someone exceptional—not just talent, skill, or education, but many things held in balance.

Returning to Chicago to star in *The First* back at the same venue where I'd had my very first professional theater job was superexciting. When I was still living in Chicago I'd often heard that the producers at the Marriott wanted to do *The First* but hadn't yet found the right actor to play Jackie Robinson. I was grateful to have been the chosen one. I'll never forget how great it felt to see my full name spelled out on the marquee: ALTON FITZGERALD WHITE STARRING AS JACKIE ROBINSON IN *THE FIRST*. I flashed back to just a few short years before when I'd driven all the way out there for an open call for *The Wiz*.

The First was the one and only musical written by the movie critic Joel Siegel. When he came to the show near the end of the run, he congratulated me, told me that Jackie would have been proud, and presented me with one of Jackie's prized baseball bats.

THE GYPSY IN MY SOUL

After finishing the run of *The First*, I headed back to New York and started my new life as a Broadway gypsy. I didn't have a job lined up and had no idea where my next paycheck would be coming from, but in the world of theater, you are never quite "unemployed." As an actor, whether you have a paying job or not, you are always working or looking for work. If you're in a show and you're smart, you are looking for ways to use it as an opportunity to land other work.

When you are not working, auditioning becomes your full-time job. You take classes, you study, you go to see your friends in shows, you work for free if you have to! And I did all those things. This keeps the muscles of your craft supple. I signed with an agency for commercial, print, and voice-over representation soon after returning to the city, and they kept me busy with auditions.

Then I got my next Broadway gig, as a replacement in *The Who's Tommy*. I was to be in the ensemble with a feature as the Hawker. I didn't want to audition for an ensemble role, but the reality of being an actor, especially a black male performer in New York City at the time, was that there were not many roles available—and I needed to work. Careers go up and down, not in a straight line. And in order to stay in the game and stay employed, I had to learn to be flexible. This is when the old saying "There are no small parts, only small actors" came into play. Whether I was doing the lead or supporting the lead as a member of the ensemble, my reputation was at stake. The truth was humbling, and the challenge for me was to find new ways to make peace with the realities of showbiz and reach a level of acceptance as soon as possible.

Meanwhile, my feelings had soured toward my agents at J. Michael Bloom. No matter how many times I asked, they were never able to get me into TV and film auditions, which I desperately wanted to pursue. After nearly pleading with them to get me seen by casting directors and even offering to go into their office and audition for them to show them that I was serious and willing, it became clear that they saw me as a stage performer only. As long as I was in a show and giving them a weekly commission, they were satisfied. They had put me in a box, and I felt powerless.

Out of frustration, I went to an open call for the *Tommy* replacement because I was tired of giving a commission to an agency that was wasn't helping me build a career. It you're talented, you'll always work someplace, but careers need to be crafted, and it's difficult to do so without a good team. I also went to the call because I missed performing and being a part of the Broadway community. The kicker came when my agents called to tell me that I had booked the show. They asked me why I hadn't told them that I was auditioning. I was honest and told them. They then informed me that even though I'd booked the job on my own, because I was signed with them, I still had to pay them a weekly commission. I was *not* happy about that!

I lasted in *Tommy* for just over a year. Then I started to get that familiar itch. As much as I enjoyed working with my castmates, I grew continually dissatisfied with having to blend in. It was a distressing feeling, because I had to constantly check in with myself as to whether my annoyance was based solely on my ego. After assessing the entire situation and my honest feelings about it, I concluded that my frustration was grounded in a passion to share in a more individual way.

It got to the point that I began to dread going to the theater and, routinely, just a few hours before show-time, my stomach would knot up. I tried talking to actor friends about how I felt, but they all warned me not to leave a Broadway show with nothing else set. I tried to explain that what I was feeling was about more than just the money. I knew that I was blessed to be one of the few black actors in a show on Broadway, and I knew that wanting to leave was completely impractical. Trust me, I was grateful, and I wanted to be satis-fied where I was. But, in my gut, I felt that something else was waiting for me. Otherwise, why couldn't I be content?

One day I got to the theater just before the half-hour call, and my stomach was acting up more than usual. I felt so emotionally drained that I couldn't even imagine performing in the show that evening. I ran down to the pay phone in the basement of the theater and called Ken Hanson, an experienced Broadway production stage manager and one of my mentors, and told him how I was feeling at that very moment. After explaining my situation to him in detail, he asked me one simple ques-tion: "Is it painful?" I thought for a second and answered, "Yes." His advice was that if that was how I truly felt, then it was probably time for me to give my notice. If

I overstayed my welcome, I could potentially infect my environment and diminish my good reputation.

When I hung up the phone, I had an instant jolt of energy knowing that I had taken back my own power. I had already saved a decent amount of money, and my plan was to concentrate on saving more in the coming months for financial and emotional security. Deciding to leave gave me a new purpose for showing up and putting even more energy into my performance. I would do the show for two more months and give my four weeks' notice to leave as a birthday present to myself in early April.

When I handed in my letter of resignation, the company was shocked. They had no idea that I was unhappy. The company manager was very sweet when I met with her to give her my letter. She told me that she thought I was great in the show and that she couldn't understand why I'd want to leave. I told her that I felt that something was waiting for me that I could not attain unless I moved on. She gave me the biggest hug and told me how much she admired me for following my instincts.

Her encouragement meant the world to me at the time because although I was excited to take the next step, I was choosing to leave a hit show to be an unemployed New York actor—and it was all based on instincts that I couldn't fully explain. The repeated questions from everyone were "Why would you leave without a job lined up?" and "What are you going to do next?" My simple answer was that it was just time for me to take a leap of faith and see what else was out there for me.

About three weeks after leaving *Tommy*, I got an audition call for *Smokey Joe's Cafe*, a new musical revue featuring the songs of Jerry Leiber and Mike Stoller, who had written some of Elvis Presley's biggest hits and created a whole catalog of standards. It was a small cast of nine principals with great highlights for each. The show had recently opened on Broadway, and the actor who was playing Ken would be leaving for three months to do a film in Europe. I went to the replacement call, along with every other black male singer/dancer in New York City, and made it down to the final three. Before I left the building, I was informed that I had gotten the role. Less than a month after leaving the ensemble of *Tommy*, I had booked another principal role on Broadway.

I had an absolute blast performing in *Smokey Joe's Cafe* for those three months. The show had the distinction of being one of the first in a new wave of jukebox musicals, and most of the reviews for it were dreadful, with some critics saying that it didn't belong on Broadway. The public, however, loved the show, and word of mouth helped turn it into a hot-ticket smash. It ultimately became Broadway's longest-running musical revue.

The downside for me was that, once again, my agency hadn't negotiated for me at all. I later found out that even the stage manager was making more money than I was, and all the other principals in the show were making thousands a week. This was the final sign that I had to find a way to get out of my contract, which still had just under a year left. And when the time came, I packed up my things and did not look back.

After my short run with *Smokey Joe's*, I went back to pounding the pavement. I focused on finding a manager who worked with only a few select clients, someone with whom I could have more attention and focus. I found that person in Renee Harriston. We clicked immediately. Our styles and visions were compatible, and she believed greatly in my potential. We began working together as I waited for my contract with J. Michael Bloom to expire.

AND THEN THERE WAS LIVENT

In the end, I severed my ties amicably with J. Michael Bloom and began working exclusively with Renee. Soon after, she got me got an audition for a company called Livent. Livent was based in Toronto and had an enormous production of *Show Boat* running on Broadway at the time. The role I was up for was that of one of the brothers in a tour of *Joseph and the Amazing Technicolor Dreamcoat* starring Donny Osmond. Livent was so fierce that they flew me to Toronto for the audition and back on the same day and even footed the bill for my meals.

The audition consisted of working with the choreographer to learn a quick dance number from the show and singing an up-tempo song and a ballad of my choice. After my work session, Garth Drabinsky, the head of Livent, came into the room to observe. He stayed for my audition, after which he said to the choreographer, "Hire him, and he'll be good for other things down the pike, too." It was known industry-wide that the next big musical Livent intended for Broadway was *Ragtime* and that several workshops had already been done.

Knowing myself, I was skeptical of taking the part in *Joseph*, so I checked in with my mentor and Broadway stage manager, Ken Hanson, about what I should do. He advised me—and we both agreed—that even though I found it challenging to go back to the ensemble, the remedy was to "count the zeros." This meant saving my money and counting the zeros in my bank account as justification for being in the ensemble. It wasn't going to be a career move. It was going to be a money move. Perceiving the job this way would afford me the opportunity and finances to plan and save for my next big career move.

I accepted the contract and joined the tour of *Joseph* in Chicago. It was "glorified ensemble," but the contract was fantastic. The salary matched if not exceeded a chorus contract on Broadway, and Livent provided a hefty per diem—a daily allowance for living costs—that in itself was enough to live on.

During put-in rehearsals for the tour in Detroit, Renee got a request for me to audition for the upcoming pre-Broadway run of *Ragtime* about to debut at the Ford Centre for the Performing Arts in Toronto (now known as the Toronto Centre for the Arts). Unlike my audition for *Joseph*, where Livent paid for my round-trip ticket, this time I would be on my own getting to and from Toronto. I had practically been wined and dined for the ensemble role in *Joseph*, yet I was given the material for Coalhouse Walker Jr. at the last minute with little time to prepare and had to find my own way to Toronto and back while already working for the company.

I had less than forty-eight hours to learn two major scenes and two lengthy songs while I was still in put-in rehearsals for *Joseph* in Detroit. The way all of it happened was so last minute that it seemed absurd. But after looking at the material and loving it, I knew that as bizarre as it all appeared, it would be worth it. I was excused from *Joseph* rehearsals for one day. I would have to be up at the crack of dawn to take a taxi across the Detroit River to the train in Windsor, Ontario, for the four-hour trip to Toronto for the audition.

After finally getting to the theater, I had a fantastic audition. I found it easy to connect with the material since it was based on the movie that had sparked my desire to become an actor. No matter how inconvenient it was getting to the audition, because of the deep desire to be a part of this work, I had to make it work. After the audition, I treated myself to lunch since I had a few hours before the four-hour train and taxi ride back to Detroit.

By the following day, word had already spread that my audition had gone well. That was encouraging. Over the next few days, though, things started turning strange. Members of the production team started to act oddly—winking at me, patting me on the back, all but congratulating me outright. After about a week of this, I pulled the associate choreographer aside for a chat. She informed me that the creative team really liked me and was probably going to be offering me a contract for *Ragtime*. This was great news, but I was praying that they didn't want me for the ensemble. The only role I was interested in was Coalhouse Walker. Even though I had a few featured moments in *Joseph*, I was still in the ensemble.

By the time the *Joseph* tour moved to Boston a few weeks later, the backstage chatter about my being in *Ragtime* had spread even further. It actually took several more weeks before Renee actually got an official call about any of it. The offer was for me to be in the ensemble and *understudy* the role of Coalhouse.

Renee thanked them for the offer and countered with my being a *standby* for the role. Livent refused, so we respectfully declined. This is where the backstage chatter at *Joseph* increased. Word had spread around now that I had been offered a contract. Everyone assumed that I would automatically accept since I was already working for the company. However, I was certain by this point that my ensemble days were going to have to come to an end. If I couldn't move forward, I wasn't going to move at all.

While *Joseph* was in Boston, I rented a basement apartment in a cousin's home in Framingham, Massachusetts. Garth Drabinsky, refusing to take my manager's *no* for an answer, bypassed her and started calling me directly. I would then call Renee and tell her what was happening, and she would tell me to "ignore him," because it was not appropriate. I couldn't believe that the head of Livent was calling me at home over an ensemble contract!

One day I was relaxing in my room on my day off when my cousin's daughter called me to the phone. It was Garth Drabinsky. I was completely caught off guard. He ranted. He raved. He insulted. He was incensed that I had turned down the ensemble role. He demeaned my manager and me for not taking advantage of this opportunity and said that we would regret it. I tried to explain to him as calmly as I could that I appreciated his offer, but that I'd reached a point in my life where it was time to craft a career for myself and that I could not be in the ensemble anymore. No matter how much I tried to explain, Garth was having none of it. I tried to end the conversation politely, thanking him again for the offer and reiterating that I simply could not be in the chorus anymore.

His reply was "Well, you're in the chorus of one of my shows right now." And my reply was "Well, Mr. Drabinsky, you will have the honor of saying that you are the last person to ever have Alton Fitzgerald White in the chorus of a show." I hung up the phone and stood there shaking. My cousin and her daughter came into the room to comfort me, because they had overheard the escalating tone of the conversation. We were all in shock and then we started laughing at how insane the whole thing seemed.

All of this made doing *Joseph* that much more challenging. Before my *Ragtime* audition, the production team at *Joseph* had already approached me about a full-time tour contract. Up to this point, I had been filling in for actors on medical leaves for three to five months at a time and with a definite end date, which made it easier for me to get through the tour. As flattered as I was to get the full-time offer, I did not want to be on the road all the time. Tired of being in the ensemble, I felt isolated in the chorus room because my cast members couldn't understand why I wouldn't want to accept the contract.

Gratefully, the universe stepped in a few weeks before Garth's climactic phone call. This time deliverance came in the form of a call from Renee about an auditioning for an upcoming London production of *Smokey Joe's Cafe*. The prospect of being cast as an original member of a West End company was extremely exciting. However, even though I had been the first replacement in the Broadway company, the creative team wanted me to audition again—for the same part! Renee was insulted and so was I, but I knew I needed to get over myself and go to the audition, so I did. New York is within reasonable driving distance from Boston, so I had plenty of time to audition and get back in time for the evening's performance of *Joseph*.

Again, every black male singer/dancer in New York City showed up for the call. During the audition, some of my pettier colleagues came at me full of questions like "What are you doing here?" and "Weren't you already in the Broadway company?" and "Why are they making you audition again?" I ignored them all, survived all the cuts, and within a few days was offered the role of Ken. I had to keep all this fantastic news to myself because I needed to give Livent four weeks' notice before leaving *Joseph*. But I had a couple of weeks left in the contract before I could officially inform them. In the meantime, I just had to deal with the discomfort of all of it.

I felt a huge amount of relief when Renee was finally able to call Livent with my notice a few weeks later.

Theater and the arts are known to be difficult paths in life, but it is true of every profession and even of our personal lives: rejection and disappointment are

unavoidable. That promotion you worked hard for and deserved will sometimes go to someone who is less qualified than you. The individual you love so much decides that he or she does not feel the same about you. People you thought were friends betray you. Businesses close and move to remote parts of the country or world. And no amount of preparation can spare you from the worst of it. You will not get through life without going through some of its worst experiences, experiences that sometimes carry enormous significance and symbolic power.

But you get to decide how you react to downturns and frustrations. You cannot let rejection and disappointment define you. No matter what is going on, you have to remember that you are more than the worst moments of your life.

To dissipate the power of disappointments and rejections, and to avoid succumbing to them, you must cultivate emotional, psychological, and spiritual tools for summoning the courage to acknowledge them rather than trying (vainly, I promise you) to ignore them. Instead, you want to move directly through, not around, them, and demonstrate to yourself and possibly others that you are greater than your misfortunes. Everyone faces challenges in life, and the mark of character is how you respond to them.

Moving through the downside of your life cycle will aid in tapping into hidden spiritual and creative resources that will keep you centered and focused on moving forward. So, expect delays in gratification and welcome them as new opportunities to learn and to exercise your own best self. Hold out for what is ultimately best suited specifically to you. Keeping your eye on the prize, no matter what happens, keeps you on course to fulfillment. And believe me when I tell you, there have been times when I have had to exert every ounce of my energy in order to move forward.

FOOD FOR THOUGHT

1. How do you react, and what do you do, when your world seems to be telling you that you are doing the right thing . . . or the wrong thing?

2. What are some of the things you can do to defuse the fear factor of trying something new?

3. Would you be ready to take over for someone if the opportunity suddenly arose? What could you do to make sure you were ready?

4. Do you earn what you think you should earn for your work? And perhaps more important, are you *valued* for your work by your employers? How do you negotiate the frequent differences between what you think you deserve and what you are being offered?

5. How could continuing your education contribute to your excelling or advancing in your chosen line of work? Are you done learning? Or are you eager to learn as much as you can?

6. Has there ever been a time when your ego got in the way of your best judgment? Have you burned bridges and acted in a way that was not in your own best interest?

7. Is there a way to learn from setbacks that can be even more potent than learning from success?

8. How do you manage to keep the challenges and successes of your own life in balance?

9. If you're feeling stuck in your job, are there ways you can take the initiative and create greater opportunities for yourself?

10. How have you reacted to rejection and disappointments in your personal and professional life? Did you surrender or take action? What does courage mean to you?

Avoid having your ego so close to your position that when your position falls, your ego goes with it.

Chapter 11

RAGTIME

Discipline and integrity are spiritual gifts that only you can give yourself. Essential to success, their benefits make it worth the hard work and tenacity required to earn them. These qualities are especially crucial when your spirit or character is challenged, either by others or by yourself. Having them at your foundation creates a healthy source of confidence that can be tapped into at any time. Being emotionally secure with a focus on the work is always more welcome than being high maintenance, insecure, and difficult to work with. The confidence gained from maintaining these virtues helps build a strong work ethic, increases your level of personal pride, and is always more attractive to others.

Performing in *Smokey Joe's Cafe* in London was a once-in-a-lifetime experience. It was exciting being a part of a theater community in another country and experiencing the similarities and differences in customs. Actors' Equity allowed the original American company to perform in London's West End for only three months, so I made the most of it, seeing every show that I could and taking advantage of London's rich history and its multitude of museums. A highlight was flying my mother, who had never been out of the United States, over to spend Thanksgiving week with me. I took her to my favorite spot for fish-and-chips, and then we crossed off a bucket list item by taking a double-decker bus tour all around London.

While I was in London, *Ragtime* began its pre-Broadway run in Toronto, and soon thereafter Livent announced that it was planning a Los Angeles company of the show. Opening a second US production before the Broadway premiere later in the fall was highly unusual, but few things regarding producer Garth Drabinsky were conventional. When I got back to New York, Renee received a call from Livent asking if I would be interested in auditioning for the West Coast company.

They assured her that I was only being considered for the role of Coalhouse Walker, and they offered to fly me out to Los Angeles for the final callbacks. After a fantastic audition, Garth pulled me into a small room and offered me the role on the spot. I was thrilled that I would finally be able to sort of originate a role. I would be the second to play it, but at least I wouldn't be replacing anyone this time. In the new Los Angeles company, I'd finally get the chance to work with the original creative team from the ground up, which was important to me at that time in my career. When you go into a show as a replacement, your rehearsals are mainly just you and a dance captain, stage manager, or associate director. It starts off as a pretty isolated experience. Over time more people are added until your final put-in rehearsal before you perform in front of an audience.

Of course, there was a complication. After congratulating me on booking the job, Garth then informed me that there was a chance that instead of opening the L.A. company, I might be going to Toronto to take over the role in that production instead. He couldn't tell me why or even when I might know. It was confusing, but I was elated to be cast in my dream role of Coalhouse Walker Jr. When I arrived back in New York after my audition, Renee began the two separate negotiations: one in case I was opening in L.A., and the other in case I was heading to Toronto. I was praying to open in Los Angeles.

The following week, while waiting to hear from Livent about their final decision regarding which *Ragtime* company I'd be joining, I first met Julie Taymor. There had been many rumors flying around about Disney doing a stage version of *The Lion King*. But no one knew whether to believe them, because as amazing as the animated feature was, putting it on a Broadway stage seemed downright impossible.

Yet sure enough, I soon got the word that *The Lion King* was casting. Even though I was already cast in

Ragtime, I decided to go to the audition. I had never auditioned for Disney and thought it would be a good idea to get myself on their radar and show Julie Taymor my work.

When I auditioned for her, I sang first. Then the two of us spent some time working together on my version of how a proud lion might carry himself. It was an unforgettable audition for me because I had never had one quite like it before or since. I hadn't ever considered how a human might portray such a commanding animal onstage in a noncomedic way.

Taymor and I seemed to click almost immediately and had a lot of fun during our session. She told me that she liked me a lot and asked me if I'd be available to be seen by the rest of the creative team in a few weeks for callbacks. I told her about my *Ragtime* situation and the possibility of my being in Canada by then. She said that she understood, congratulated me, and then told me that she looked forward to seeing me again for the show, hopefully in the near future. I was thrilled that she was interested.

A few days later I got that call from Livent. I would be going to Toronto. I had about a week to pack up my life, get my affairs in order, and move to Canada for seven months. Livent helped me find a great apartment near downtown but on the train line to the theater.

During my first evening in Toronto, I was finally given a ticket to see the show. It was kind of surreal sitting in the audience waiting to see a production I had already signed a contract for but knew so little about. *Ragtime* was magnificent, visually cinematic, and huge in scope. I couldn't believe that I was about to share the stage with Tony Award nominees Marin Mazzie and Peter Friedman, and play opposite Tony Award winner Audra McDonald as Sarah. I didn't know until I saw the show that Coalhouse takes the last bow, which is reserved for the star of the show. It was thrilling, watching and knowing that I was about to be a part of something so incredible.

My rehearsals with the dance captain and associate director began the next day. I soaked it all up enthusiastically, and I retained the information quickly. After a few days, principal understudies were brought in to work with me, including Audra's cover, Heather Headley, who went on to originate the role of Nala in *The Lion King* and then the title role in Disney's *Aida*, for which she won a Tony Award for Best Actress in a Musical. Heather and I became "train buddies." We would often ride the train together back toward town after the show.

I was so far ahead in rehearsals that the team gave me five days off and told me to be back in time for my final put-in rehearsal. I took the time to fly back to New York City to get more of my belongings, see some shows, and continue celebrating with friends. My only concern with my put-in was driving the show's Ford Model T onstage. It had to fit into a very narrow wing, and I wouldn't be able to practice until that day. After returning, my put-in rehearsal went smoothly and I made my debut as Coalhouse that same evening.

When I opened in Toronto, not a single member of the creative team was there. They had already moved on to Los Angeles to begin preparations and rehearsals there. I was grateful to be working and playing such an amazing part, but felt let down that I was going into the show without any direct access to the creative team. I was performing the male lead in a gigantic show, but I felt more like a replacement than ever before.

Renee and I had to nearly beg for a meeting with the writers, director, and choreographer of *Ragtime*. Renee finally convinced them to come to Canada for a one-day work session. The writers acknowledged that my voice was a little higher than my predecessor's, so they raised the keys. I had more of a dance background, so the choreographer gave me more movement for "Gettin' Ready Rag," a big number where Coalhouse makes the decision to go in search of his love, Sarah. This helped give me more of a solid foundation in the show. And I was grateful.

I was having the time of my life, but members of the cast seemed unhappy. They weren't cold, but they were not terribly welcoming either. Thankfully, some of the cast members invited me out for drinks and filled me in on the drama. Apparently, Livent had announced the West Coast company without informing any of them. With the exception of two members of the Toronto company who were allowed to join the California production, the rest of them were contracted to stay in Canada for the entire run and then go straight to Broadway in the fall, where a theater (now called the Lyric) was being rehabbed for the opening. A whole new set of actors in Los Angeles would actually get the US premiere while they, the cast that cocreated the show, were all basically stuck in Toronto.

I was told that some of them had found out about the situation when friends started calling them for audition tips about roles they were already playing. I also learned that before I arrived on the scene in Canada, Coalhouse's understudy was made to believe that *he* would be taking over the role, so I was viewed as the outsider who was hired out of nowhere to come in, take over the lead, and disrupt the original family. My castmates apologized for their lack of enthusiasm for my joining the company, but I totally understood how betrayed they must have felt. This realization helped to thin the air a bit, and we all seemed more comfortable afterward.

Near the end of the Toronto run, Livent extended an offer for me to take over the lead role in Los Angeles. My negotiations went very smoothly, and as a last-minute request and almost as an afterthought, Renee and I asked to have first refusal for the Broadway company in my contract. We thought it wouldn't be a big deal, but Garth blew his top and refused to grant it. That he was so adamant about it made us suspicious, especially knowing how he'd handled the Los Angeles situation with the Toronto cast. Garth finally asked if the right of first refusal was a deal-breaker, and Renee and I agreed that it was. Having first refusal was my only guarantee of security. All my negotiations had gone smoothly up to that point and we were expecting him to agree.

After a week of not hearing a thing from Livent, I answered a panicked call from Renee asking me if I was sitting down. She'd received a call from the resident director of *Ragtime* asking how I was taking the news. Of course, Renee didn't know what she was talking about. Apparently, Garth was so furious about the first-refusal request that he immediately called the original Toronto understudy and offered him the role in L.A. He did this without even the courtesy of informing us that he had moved on.

It also occurred to me that my fellow cast members had known this for at least a week before I did, and no one had said a thing to me about it. I felt angry, hurt, and betrayed—but also a little relieved. When I got to the theater that night, I asked the understudy if he'd please stop by my dressing room at intermission. He hesitantly agreed. When he came by, I congratulated him on getting the role, wished him all the very best in Los Angeles, and told him how happy I was for him that he was going to have the chance to make the role his own. He was a bit stunned, but I sincerely meant what I said to him.

Even before the first refusal became an issue, I just couldn't envision myself doing the show in Los Angeles. I missed New York and didn't want to be away from home for another year. Financially, it would have been great, but artistically I wasn't looking forward to being a replacement yet again and jumping onto another already fully running machine. The circumstances that led to the final outcome were far from ideal, but the end result felt like some kind of divine order.

Before the Canada run ended, Livent threw the company a huge party with announcements that the theater would indeed be finished in time for the first preview on Broadway a few months later. It was the first time that anyone in the company had seen Garth in months, and I had definitely not seen him since my negotiations had broken down. Even though things were ending in a way that was less than ideal and, for me, unresolved, I wanted to thank him face-to-face for the phenomenal opportunity to play Coalhouse in such an unforgettable show. But every time I tried to get his attention, he seemed to avoid me.

I finally got to him and extended my hand to say thank you. He ignored my gesture and immediately began tearing into me about what a mistake I'd made putting the "demand" of first refusal on him, how I had blown the chance of a lifetime, and how I would never work for Livent again. I was stunned and tried to keep my composure, but when he began to raise his voice and speak more inappropriately, to the point of attracting attention, I interrupted him, said that I only wanted to thank him, and then walked away as his voice continued to trail and holler after me. I stepped outside to get some fresh air. I was trembling.

After the closing, I went back to New York, where word quickly spread that I had been fired from *Ragtime*. As crazy and embarrassing as it all felt, the fact is that I had turned down the contract. When my theater colleagues stopped gossiping and whispering long enough to actually ask me, I told them simply that Livent had made me an offer that I felt I could refuse—and so I had refused it. Only my close friends believed me. It was a difficult time, but I was relieved that my integrity was intact and proud that I'd stood up for myself.

AFTER *RAGTIME* BLUES

After being back in the city for a few weeks, I decided to fly to Los Angeles to meet with a casting director I had met in Toronto during the last week of my *Ragtime* run. We met in her office on the 20th Century Fox lot. We connected immediately, and the next thing I knew, she was on her phone calling around town to set up meetings for me with agents for representation. This woman seemed determined to find a place for me in television. My weeklong trip turned into three weeks of meetings until I settled on a midsize agency that she highly recommended. I made the decision almost every actor makes at one point or another in their career: I decided to move to L.A.

I flew back home with three months to prepare for my move to Los Angeles for TV pilot season in January. A friend who would be away for a month let me sublet his studio apartment in the San Fernando Valley, and I rented a car at the airport in hopes of finding a used car to purchase soon after. It was exciting and scary being in a new city where I had few acquaintances. *Ragtime* was playing in L.A., and there were posters and advertisements everywhere, which was a bit tough to swallow. Livent was also in the midst of conducting auditions for an upcoming national tour of the show, and in the weeks leading up to my move west, I was flooded with calls from colleagues auditioning for the show looking for tips, which I had no problem giving them. I gave them the best advice I could and wished them well.

Unfortunately, I lasted less than a month in L.A. before all hell broke loose and I reached my breaking point. In my first few days there, I got food poisoning for the first time in my life and was as sick as a dog with no friends or family around to help. My monthlong sublet had only lasted about a week when my friend had an unexplained emergency that meant he needed to return to his very small studio immediately. After repacking my things and loading them in the rental car, another sublet that I thought I'd secured fell through overnight, leaving me no choice but to rent a room at a motel. On top of that, I missed my first couple of auditions. This was before cell phones became the norm, and pagers were the fastest way to reach someone; but I had difficulty getting the hang of what was, to me, new technology. By the time I'd get the message and return the call at a *pay phone (!)*, it would be too late to get to the other side of town to make the appointments. I was not off to a good start.

The daily car rental got expensive. But to prove to the universe that I was serious about making Los Angeles work despite the challenges, I took the leap and purchased a car. I answered an ad about expert mechanics who take you to car auctions for repossessed cars to bid on at low prices. I won and purchased a beautiful 1974 VW Beetle, one of my dream cars. My mechanic checked it out, fixed it up, and had it ready for me in a few days. However, just when I returned the rental car and thought that I could move on, the VW started having multiple mechanical problems that peaked after my second week in the L.A. While driving home late one evening, just as I was about to enter the fast lane of the 101 freeway, my car started sputtering.

I had barely enough time to exit the highway and get onto local streets. I prayed that the car would hold out until I got to the motel I was staying in, which was on the other side of a steep hill in the Valley. The VW made it about a quarter of the way up before it started smoking and eventually stopped running, leaving me just enough momentum to turn the car around and glide back down.

I was terrified. This was around the time that Ennis Cosby, Bill Cosby's only son, had had car trouble on the freeway and wound up being murdered. It was past midnight; I had no close friends in the area and no cell phone. All that I could do was pray that I wouldn't have to stop at a red light, as I was afraid that I'd never get the car started again. Tears of fear and exhaustion ran down my face.

For some reason, I had noticed in Los Angeles that I'd often see cars parked at gas stations. I thought it peculiar and wondered why I'd even taken notice of it. As I coasted down the hill through two miraculously green traffic lights, I approached a gas station at the bottom of the hill and noticed a bunch of cars parked with only one space open, directly in front of where the gas pump was. My car had just enough momentum to make it up the entrance ramp, past the pump, and right into the only spot available. Had there been a car pumping gas in that spot, I wouldn't have made it without needing a push. There was no question in my mind: it was a miracle.

After parking, I spoke with the gas station attendant, who informed me that I would need to come back in the morning to talk to someone about fixing the car or towing it to another location. I asked him how I could get a taxi from there to the San Fernando Valley. He directed me around the corner to a hotel. I nearly gasped when I arrived there and realized that it was the same Hilton Hotel where Livent had housed me when they'd flown me out for my *Ragtime* callback! I immediately knew that it was more than just a coincidence. Just being familiar with the place took some of the edge off the whole miserable experience.

I went on to spend more money in the next few days on taxis, towing, and visiting apartments for a possible roommate or sublet situation. Los Angeles was not being kind. And I was becoming depressed. No matter how much I tried, I couldn't even seem to get started.

A week later, after more car trouble and a long day of apartment hunting, I walked into my motel room to the sound of the phone ringing. It was Renee calling to inform me that Livent had called. They couldn't find a Coalhouse to their liking, and Annie, the associate director, wanted to talk to me about possibly playing the role again. I told Renee to give her my number.

Annie called me and immediately started selling me on the tour with names of costars and assurances that the creative team would be there to build the new production together. Rehearsals would begin in New York in a couple of weeks. If only she'd known my present situation. I was elated to do the role again, and I suddenly realized why the universe wouldn't let me get comfortable in Los Angeles.

The entire time I was in L.A., in every car I rented (and even at my temporary sublet), the cassette player wouldn't work, so I couldn't listen to my personal favorite tunes. I found myself singing more than normal, and usually a cappella. I realized that even if I had booked a TV show or something, I would have missed singing, and that my passion to share my talents in that way was actually the most important thing to me at the time.

In the end, I realized that the universe had sent me to Los Angeles to detach from my NYC life and have a break from the humiliation of the rumors about being fired. But the intention was never for me to stay in L.A.

Annie thought that I might still have hard feelings about how things had ended in Toronto. Of course my feelings were hurt, but I put on my "business hat," which helps me separate myself from my emotions. I thanked her for the call and then suggested that she call Renee and work it out. Within a few hours, Renee called me back with the deal completely done, including first refusal for Broadway. I called my mother with the great news and then went immediately to UPS to send all my boxes back to New York City!

The *Ragtime* tour opened at the legendary National Theatre in Washington, DC, on April 14, 1998. Putting the tour together with the original team was another realized dream. I was able to put my own stamp on Coalhouse and loved working together with the entire cast. But there was yet another "snag" ahead. After being under investigation for its business practices,

225

Livent filed for bankruptcy. The week before we were to move from Minneapolis to Seattle, we were informed that the tour would end that week. The cast was in total shock. We had already shipped our trunks filled with our belongings ahead and secured apartments in Seattle. We were told that another company was in talks with Actors' Equity to work out a deal to take over the tour, but that no information could be specified for a few days. Everyone was panicked and heartbroken.

The very next day, Renee called. I was expecting more bad news, but she informed me that I was on my way back to New York to take over the role of Coalhouse on Broadway and that my wonderful new deal was already negotiated. I was ecstatic, of course, yet conflicted because my fellow cast members were distraught about the tour folding. I decided it was best to keep my great news to myself. Thankfully, the very next day, the company got confirmation that the deal with Equity had gone through and that the tour would continue. Talk about a roller coaster of a week!

After closing in Seattle, I went into *Ragtime* on Broadway and crossed another item off my professional wish list by playing opposite the wonderful actress LaChanze. She was a future Tony winner for her role as Celie in *The Color Purple*. But a few years before that, she had taken over the role of Sarah in *Ragtime*.

I'd had a huge crush on her and been a fan of hers since seeing her in *Once on This Island* on Broadway over a dozen times! I had only worked with LaChanze for a short time when she left the company to begin maternity leave. Happily, Darlesia Cearcy, my Sarah from the national tour, stepped in for LaChanze.

Nothing lasts forever, the saying goes, and my good spirits took a huge hit a few months later.

STORMY WEATHER: REALITY BITES

On July 16, 1999, I was arrested by the NYPD, along with three young men who had just graduated from college and were moving into my building in Manhattan. It was moving day for them, and I had just given them a great tour of the building and bragged about how safe it was. When we entered the lobby on our way out, we passed two young guys speaking Spanish on their cell phones. I had never seen them before, and the only thing that struck me was that I could never get cell phone reception in my lobby as they seemed to have.

As we approached the exit, I could see a couple of what I thought were paramedics trying to get in. There were a number of elderly tenants in my building, and, concerned that it might be an emergency, I hurried ahead to unlock the door and let them into the building. When I opened the door, I realized that they were the police. I greeted them politely, and the next thing I knew, the four of us were all pushed against a wall in the vestibule, stripped of our belongings, searched, and made to drop to our knees with our hands behind our backs, and then handcuffed while they searched my backpack. I didn't know my heart could pound so hard.

There was no explanation. We were all in a small space between the street door and the locked lobby door. The police wanted to get into the lobby, so I offered to get off my knees and let them use my key to unlock the door. The two strangers we'd passed in the lobby were the ones the police were looking for. I thought that at any second, they would just let us go and apologize for their terrible mistake.

No such luck. A small crowd had gathered both inside and outside of the building. The NYPD then took us outside and put the actual criminals and us in two separate cars, ignoring my neighbors who tried to vouch for my character and pleaded with the cops to release me.

When we got to the Thirty-Second Precinct, the two criminals were immediately recognized for prior crimes, and I thought again that we'd be released. Instead we were thrown in jail alongside them and strip-searched. It was surreal. Five hours later, we were finally released. I missed my evening performance of *Ragtime*. The precinct's excuse was that we were at the wrong place at the wrong time. Rejecting their lame attempt at an apology, my reply was "I was where I live." The four of us walked back to the building in a complete daze. I felt like Coalhouse in real life. We had just experienced life imitating art in the worst way.

Before we were stopped and arrested, the three new graduates had been about to unpack a truck full of their belongings for their move, and I had been on my way to the bank. The three graduates hadn't even been allowed to lock their van before they took us all away! In my backpack, which was repeatedly searched, I had a few weeks of payroll checks totaling nearly $10,000. Was I racially profiled? Were they jealous that I had so much money on me? Did they keep us just because they could, even though none of us fit the description of young light-skinned Hispanics? It was *I* who had helped *them* get into *my* building! My head was spinning with questions that could not be answered.

The press found out, and the story broke on the local news later that evening. It quickly spread nationally with headlines like BROADWAY STAR MISTAKENLY ARRESTED AND RACIALLY PROFILED. It was a top story that was trumped only by the unfortunate news starting to come in of John F. Kennedy Jr.'s plane crash the previous evening.

It took me several days before I could get my head together and get back to the show and deal with the racial aspects of the event—and with the fact that as Coalhouse, I was being called a nigger by other characters onstage at every performance. I was experiencing feelings virtually identical to those of the character Coalhouse, except that he had dealt with them in the early 1900s, and mine were nearly a century later. The show took on a new and deeper meaning for me, making me even more committed to emotionally investing in the character of Coalhouse and his pursuit of justice.

Norman Siegel from the American Civil Liberties Union (ACLU) called me to discuss pursuing a case against the NYPD. After meditating on it, I decided I would be honored to have them represent me. Norman told me to come up with a dollar amount to sue them for and assured me that no matter how large or small the number I chose, I would probably not get it. Getting the NYPD to financially compensate me was not my motivation. Justice and calling attention to the issue of racial profiling were.

I decided on $750,000, because a million felt gratuitous. When the newspapers printed the amount, I immediately received phone calls and e-mails about properties for sale, requests for donations, and congratulations on winning so much money. It was ludicrous. All that anyone seemed to focus on or talk about—and write about—was the money. Because of the amount printed, people to this very day believe that I won millions of dollars in my case and are convinced that it's how I purchased property in Harlem. Apparently, it was hard to believe I could be a homeowner due to hard work, careful saving, smart investing, and strategic planning. More than a dozen years later, I asked a couple of new acquaintances if they'd ever heard any rumors about my winning a case, and they confided that they had. From what they told me, the dollar amounts that I am rumored to have won range from $2 million to $3.5 million. It's as if suing the NYPD had meant they simply told me to name my price and then just gave it to me, all without even a trial. I knew that in reality there was no money to be had, and I am grateful that although the incident hurt me deeply, I was intuitive enough to realize that it provided me an opportunity to be of service and to serve as an example.

People were actually shocked that this could happen to an African American "Broadway star" who was an upstanding citizen with an excellent reputation. Norman and I took advantage of the press and did practically every television program that invited us for interviews, including a profile on NBC's *Dateline*. I knew that I now had a platform on which to share my story and only a limited time in which to do it. I could speak about the mistaken arrest calmly and clearly in ways that anyone of any race or ethnicity could relate to.

The Nation, a magazine that I'd never heard of, called about an interview. I was irritated with how the media and public were spinning my story, focusing on the dollar amount, and told the magazine that I was only interested if they'd let me write my own article. They agreed to let me have a shot. I wrote it and passed it along to Renee to proofread, and she sent it to the magazine.

The Nation liked it, made some edits, and asked me for a head shot. Two months later my head shot was on the cover of the magazine with my article titled "Ragtime, My Time." The article I wrote has since been reprinted countless times in publications all over the country and is published in dozens of college textbooks for its structure and content, so some good came out of a very bad experience. It was a very difficult time for me, but I knew that it was a service that I was specifically meant to do, given my position in *Ragtime*. It made perfect sense given my deep personal connection to the movie, which had inspired me to choose my life's profession so many years before when I was still in high school.

Another dream came true for me when the new producers of *Ragtime* decided on a fresh marketing plan for the show with a commercial and a poster in which I was prominently featured.

Ragtime closed on Broadway in January 2000. And by that point, I was completely burned out. I turned down lots of work and auditions for the next several months to rest and focus on restoring and renovating the property I'd recently purchased and rehabilitating my spirit. The press from the incident had died down a bit, and I tried to detach from all of it as much as I could, knowing that it would be a long, hard road ahead pursuing my case against the NYPD.

In this imperfect world of ours, chances are that your

character will be challenged in some way or another. Even those of us who strive to do the right thing and surround ourselves with a loving support group of friends and family will run into problems. No one is perfect. Invariably, some people will mistake your motives, and others will maliciously or jealously try to tear you down by lying about you and your behavior. And this can be in the professional or interpersonal arena.

If, after reflection, we realize that we are wrong about something, the best and first thing to do is apologize for what we believe to have been our responsibility. Sometimes the reaction is positive, sometimes it's not, and sometimes it's a mix of both. We should keep ourselves as open to criticism as possible and acknowledge that people who feel wronged by us might have a point or two. It's easy to accept criticism if you keep the focus on behavior rather than essence. If your behavior has been less than ideal, accept it and try to change. But don't let people attack you for what or who you are. "I did not like what you did" is not the same kind of challenge as "I do not like who you are."

If you keep the focus of your life on your good character and stay on your best behavior, you will be immune to attacks on your core identity. Your faith in who you are can protect you from others projecting their ideas and definitions of who they think you are or *try to make you out to be. It can be dumbfounding to be accused of something by another person, because sometimes you couldn't have come up with the motives they are ascribing to you if your life depended on it. It just isn't you. Reminder: it's probably them.*

The ability to exercise the courage to be honest and responsible for your actions and choices feeds the maturity of your spirit and leads to greater confidence and self-awareness. Full accountability and self-knowledge build strong character that cannot be disputed by anyone. And although you may find yourself in dismaying circumstances, your essential self is untouchable.

FOOD FOR THOUGHT

1. How is it possible to accept something with gratitude even when it is not what you really want?

2. What skills, traits, and attributes can you foster to survive when chaos seems to reign all around you, and when you just have to wait for other people to make decisions that greatly impact your life?

3. Have you ever felt that you had to decide between standing up for yourself or backing down and accepting something you thought was unfair or otherwise unacceptable? How do you know what to do?

4. How do you choose between money and growth in a particular situation? Neither is wrong, but does one sometimes seem more or less acceptable?

5. Have you ever felt that your life is in some kind of divine order? What does that mean to you? Or, if not, what would it take for you to consider the possibility that everything is as it should be today?

6. Have you ever just felt that life was trying to tell you something?

7. How important is integrity in the scheme of your work and personal life? How can it help sustain you in a crisis?

8. What are the costs of bitterness?

To be nobody-but-yourself—in a world which is doing its best, night and day, to make you everybody else—means to fight the hardest battle which any human being can fight; and never stop fighting.

—E. E. Cummings, poet

Chapter 12

MY *LION KING*

Whatever your occupation is, reconceiving it as a form of service can change your entire approach to your job and your life. And it's one of the most liberating things you can do for yourself. Your job becomes something you do for others instead of something you do for yourself. While many fear that one's essential self becomes lost in service to others, the opposite is true: service is a way to greater self-discovery. Just as making a commitment is sometimes harder than keeping it, defining your life's work as service does not make it feel more onerous. Rather, it motivates you to greater and more energetic contributions, from which you receive great rewards.

Even before I saw Disney's *The Lion King* on Broadway, I was admittedly biased. I was on tour with *Ragtime* while both shows were competing for the 1998 Tony Award for Best Musical, and of course, *The Lion King* won. After calling every contact that I had to get one of the hottest tickets in town, I finally got to see it. I immediately understood why *The Lion King* won. Like everyone else on the planet, I became a fan. It was theatrically thrilling! The cast, music, voices, puppets, and costumes were the most incredible ear and eye candy I had ever witnessed.

A couple of months after *Ragtime*'s closing on Broadway (in January 2000), I got a call from Disney to audition for the Los Angeles production of *The Lion King*. It was great to see Julie Taymor again, but I went into my audition feeling conflicted. Still exhausted from my *Ragtime* experience, I wasn't yet ready to commit to the discipline that eight shows a week require, and I wasn't comfortable moving to the West Coast while I was still deep in the throes of construction on my home—the first I'd ever owned.

In addition, with the impending court case still looming, I felt uneasy about the possibility of being away for a year. I was eager to be a part of the Disney family, but they weren't keen on less than a one-year commitment. Knowing that I wasn't physically and emotionally available, my gut said that it was better to bow out gracefully to avoid potentially burning a major bridge down the road. So, I respectfully declined the invitation to the callback.

A year later, Disney called again, this time for *The Lion King*'s national tour—the Gazelle Tour, as it was called, which is still touring to this day. Matters regarding my court case were moving slowly, but my home renovation was nearly complete. I was ready to get back to my theater work. I reviewed and studied the Mufasa material, had a pre-callback work session with Jeff Lee, the show's amazing associate director, and then went before Julie and the creative team for the final callback. After my audition, Julie asked me, "Are we finally gonna do this?" I chuckled and answered, "I sure hope so!" And just like that, my *Lion King* journey began. I was ecstatic!

Rehearsals for the tour were at 890 Broadway, on the exact same floor where I'd rehearsed *Miss Saigon*. The cast for the tour consisted mostly of performers who had never done the show, and it was great building a fresh new production together. Just weeks before I left New York for the tour, my lawyer (and the head of the ACLU), Norman Siegel, called to tell me that the city wanted to settle the case with an informal apology and a very small sum of money, all of which I donated to the ACLU. It was a tremendous relief to have the case closed, and one less thing to worry about before I left town to begin a wonderful new chapter on the road.

It had taken Disney a few years to create a traveling *Lion King* that could live up to the Broadway production. So, when it finally went out on the road, cities that weren't near New York or Los Angeles were starving for it. In the weeks leading up to the first performance, at the Buell Theatre in Denver on April 21, 2002, there were lines around the block for tickets, and every performance was like being in a rock concert. The audiences would scream and applaud during the opening "Circle of Life" scene with its procession of "animals" through the audience, and then jump to their feet immediately during the curtain call. The entire cast knew that we were blessed to be a part of a once-in-a-lifetime phenomenon, and we were thrilled to be the first to take it on the road.

It was during our glorious eight-week gig in Fort Lauderdale, Florida, that I discovered something about myself. It was the most time I'd ever spent that close to the ocean, and I was at the water every single day we were there—walking, jogging, sunbathing, or just staring out at the Atlantic in meditation. Up until that point, I had no idea how much I loved the ocean waves and how spiritually healing it was for me. It calmed me and energized me at the same time. It was wonderful to discover that the ocean was available to me anytime

I needed a revitalizing sanctuary. The mountains had always done that for me; now I was discovering the healing nature of the sea.

A major highlight of the tour was playing Mufasa in my hometown. The tour's first stop in Cincinnati was in the spring of 2003. I never knew when I came out of the stage door after each show what surprise would be waiting: old friends, teachers, relatives and acquaintances—people from every stage of my childhood, adolescence, and early career. Their exclamations of pride and joy were almost overwhelming.

Many of my dreams were realized while I was in Cincinnati with the show. I performed a benefit concert at my alma mater, the School for Creative and Performing Arts, and set up a scholarship fund for students who couldn't afford private voice lessons. I had benefited from a similar kind of scholarship when I was a student at the school, so having the opportunity to give back felt wonderful. Being able to be of service and perform on the very same stage where it all began for me was surreal.

I conducted several master classes and did a few Q and A sessions at the school. I was invited to give the commencement address for the school's class of 2003, where I sang "The Impossible Dream" and spoke about no dream being too impossible to achieve with discipline, passion, and focus. An extra treat was fulfilling my childhood fantasy of riding in a parade downtown and waving to the crowd as a member of the procession for the Cincinnati Reds' Opening Day festivities.

THE KING IS DEAD: LONG LIVE THE KING

I was extremely grateful that I had the opportunity to spend more time with my family than I had since I left for Chicago. It was a gift to have the time to reconnect with them on a deeper, more adult level. While I was in Cincinnati, we unexpectedly lost two family members. My mother's father, Thomas Cody, had been in a nursing home in declining health. When he passed away, I was able to grieve with my mother and sisters. The other death was particularly unexpected. It was my father.

Several months before the tour played Cincinnati, while we were in Dallas, I was on a long scenic drive, and out of the clear blue I began obsessively thinking about what it was going to be like being in my hometown for eight weeks. I thought about my childhood and how far I had come spiritually in terms of healing the wounds of my childhood, especially the absence of a close relationship with my father. By then, with the help of therapy, prayer, meditation, and even playing Mufasa, *The Lion King*'s iconic father, my feelings toward my own father had shifted from anger to sympathy to forgiveness.

I now had personal experience regarding the many challenges adults face, especially men of color. Like many black men of his generation, my father had a fraction of the options afforded me, and his addiction to alcohol hadn't made it any easier for him. Age and experience had given me a new compassion and respect for my father.

While driving and meditating that afternoon in Dallas, it suddenly occurred to me that I had never spent a full afternoon alone with him since I'd become an adult. The more I thought about it, the more urgent the feeling became, so I pulled over and called him to make a date six months in the future when I would be in Cincinnati. He sounded hesitant and a bit timid on the phone, but I assured him that we could do whatever he wanted to do; that we could just sit in a restaurant and have a meal. I tried to explain that I just wanted to spend some time with him.

Six months later with the show in Cincinnati, that day arrived. Excited about the afternoon, I called to see if my father was ready for me to pick him up. My sister Darlene, with whom he shared a home, answered the phone and told me that he wasn't feeling well and would have to cancel. She apologized for him and, hearing the disappointment in my voice, asked if I was okay. She knew how much I had been looking forward to it.

Needless to say, I was disappointed and hurt. My father was rarely sick, and the little boy in me wondered if it was just an excuse to avoid spending an afternoon with me. Thankfully, after processing my feelings and detaching from my childhood hurt, my adult self was satisfied that I had at least extended the invitation. Unfortunately, my father was taken to the hospital later that evening and diagnosed with emphysema among other things. He was released after a few days, but he was eventually readmitted.

My mother couldn't get enough of *The Lion King* so

I had arranged a ticket for her (for probably the tenth time). At around 4:00 P.M. on the day of the show, she called to tell me that my father's condition was declining and asked if there was a way to cancel the ticket. I assured her that it would be no problem since the show was selling out every night. At that point, I hadn't yet gone to the hospital to see my father, and my mother repeatedly suggested that I do so. It bothered me that even with the emphysema diagnosis, my father was said to have continued to sneak out and smoke.

My excuse for not going to see him was that, despite the family's concern for him, he chose to ignore his doctor's orders and do whatever he wanted—as always. Plus, my father was almost never ill and would probably be back home shortly. Perhaps I was still hurt because of the lunch cancellation. As hard as I tried not to, I was judging him, but after hearing the unease in my mother's voice, I decided that I would visit him immediately after the show that evening.

I got into my makeup and costume and took my place backstage for the opening number, as I had many times before. But right after the first note of the show, I suddenly knew that something was off. As I was climbing Pride Rock as Mufasa during "The Circle of Life," I had to fight back tears and couldn't understand why. When I got to the scene between Mufasa and Simba that leads into "They Live in You," I could barely keep it together. When I sang the song to Simba that evening as a father to his son, it felt as if I was hearing the lyrics for the first time after already having sung it hundreds of times before. I sincerely had no idea what was wrong with me.

I had barely made it offstage when I nearly collapsed from the heaviness. When I got to my dressing room, I called Renee to tell her what was going on with my father, and she told me to leave the theater immediately. I said that I couldn't because I still had another scene to do before intermission, and she all but demanded that I go right to stage management to tell them that my father was gravely ill and that I had to go right away. Renee is the only person who could have convinced me to do this, because she too had unresolved issues with her father, which we'd discussed many times. I did what she said, washed off the makeup, changed my clothes, and made my way to the hospital.

When I walked into my father's hospital room, my mother's eyes lit up. She and Darlene, my youngest sister, were at his bedside. There were lots of tubes, machines, and monitors. His breathing was heavy, as if he were literally fighting off death. My mother said that the doctors had given him only a few more hours to live, but the moment she said it, I knew that he would pass away within the next few minutes and that he had been waiting for me to come. I cannot explain how I knew this, but I felt it deeply and was 100 percent sure. After a few minutes, his breathing suddenly calmed and seemed to normalize. My mother and sister sat down on chairs near the front of his bed while I stood as we started sharing funny stories about him to lighten the mood.

At one point in the conversation, for no reason in particular and as if on cue, my attention abruptly shifted to the monitors. The numbers were going down. It was slow at first and then began to speed up. My mother and sister were still chatting when I announced that the time was near. They both looked at me with astonished looks on their faces. A few seconds later bells and alarms started going off, and nurses and doctors ran into the room. The entire time I was in the hospital room, it seemed as if I knew everything that was going to happen a few seconds before it did.

After being such a wreck at the theater, I couldn't believe how calm I was. The three of us gathered around him and told him that it was okay to let go. I stroked his hand and said to him with absolute gratitude and sincerity, "You may have not been the perfect father, Paul W. White, but thank you so very much for having me." A few seconds later, his breathing got slower and slower, and then there was a final exhale. It was sad, bittersweet, fascinating, and unforgettable.

When I looked at the clock, it was just a few minutes past eleven. If I had come after the show, as I had originally planned, I would have missed him. I knew in my heart that his spirit had come to me at the theater and that I was so unusually emotional during the show because he was calling me to him. His physical body had waited for me to be there with him at his bedside.

I had always wondered what it would be like to be away from home and get a call that my father was no longer with us. Addiction can lead a person into dangerous situations, and there is nothing you can do to stop addicts from trying to satisfy their need, no matter how much you love them and worry about them. Because of our strained relationship, I didn't think I'd feel much of anything when I got that call. Having been there to see him take his final breath, though, I cannot imagine having been anyplace else in the world but there with him.

A WHOLE NEW WORLD

Way back during the first week of rehearsals for *The Lion King* tour, the creative team joked that the principals were so talented and worked so well together that we'd probably all eventually be in the show on Broadway. I didn't think much of it beyond being flattered, but near the end of the first year of the tour, two principals were offered replacement roles in the Broadway company. It is difficult when an original-cast family begins to break up and its members leave for other opportunities, especially when you're traveling together. On tour, you tend to rely on one another in deeper ways than you do with a stationary company. On tour, you become more dependent on the consistency of your friendships and connections in the company to keep you grounded and stable as you travel from city to city.

Soon there were three principals leaving for New York, and before I knew it, I was the fourth to receive an offer. I couldn't believe that I was going to have the opportunity to perform such an iconic role in a smash hit show that was still selling out every night on Broadway and setting one box office record after another. My last time on Broadway, I had been one of the leads in *Ragtime*, which was directly across the street from the New Amsterdam on Forty-Second Street, where *The Lion King* was playing. I would often look across the street at the marquee and think about how the roles of Coalhouse Walker Jr. and King Mufasa were the two best roles on Broadway at the time (especially for black actors) and how amazing it would be to play Mufasa there one day. After all the false-arrest drama that clouded the end of my experience in *Ragtime*, this offer gave me the opportunity to go back to Broadway under much happier circumstances.

Performing on the New Amsterdam stage was a treat, not only creatively but visually, too: it is truly the most magnificent of all the Broadway theaters. The view from the stage was spectacular with all the gorgeous intricate carvings and stunning details out where the audience sits. And although *The Lion King* is a massive show, the size and shape of the theater make the performances feel wonderfully cozy and intimate. In 2006, Disney moved the show from the New Amsterdam a few blocks north to the Minskoff Theatre to make room for its upcoming production of *Mary Poppins*. Being in a show that was moving from one Broadway house to another felt like being on tour, but still staying in NYC. It was fun rehearsing as a full cast and rediscovering the show as we made the transition.

In connection with the move, Disney decided to do a new marketing campaign for the show. It included a new commercial featuring . . . wait for it: me! The ad showed me in the makeup chair getting my face painted, then me getting dressed as Mufasa and having my mask put into place, and then me in full costume in the wings preparing to enter the stage. It was a tremendous honor to have been chosen as the so-called "face of *The Lion King*."

After nearly three years in the Broadway company, I was happy, but starting to feel a bit restless. This concerned me. I still loved my job, but *creatively* I was beginning to grow tired of my routine. I didn't want to burn any bridges or sabotage my wonderful relationship with Disney, so I knew that I needed to find new incentive to continue to grow in the show as well as personally (and maybe even beyond that).

My first solution was to focus more on gratitude and constantly remind myself how blessed I was to be a working actor, doing what I loved, and making a great living at it in the theater capital of the world. I also increased the lending of my talents to benefit concerts, readings, and workshops of new projects. This enabled me to stay busy outside of the show while keeping my creative skills sharpened.

Since I was now back in the city and comfortable, I decided that it was a good time to get back into therapy. I had developed great discipline regarding my body and my career and thought it was time to work on maintaining my positive mental health. I had seen a therapist years before to help resolve issues with my father and my childhood so that I could spend less time dreading the past and more time being in the beautiful present moments I was experiencing. It was important for me to find a therapist with whom I could develop a deep relationship. I hoped to meet a good, skilled listener whom I could trust to help me continue moving forward in my life. I also knew that it was time for me to get back to Al-Anon, the twelve-step program for relatives and friends of alcoholics to share their experience, strength, and hope in order to solve their common problems.

Dealing with my father's alcoholism contributed to my overachieving in both a positive and negative sense. Even with my many successes, I sometimes felt powerless over my need to go beyond the call of duty and overcompensate because of my lack of confidence in some areas. Few people knew, but my success and constant busyness (my workaholism) enabled me to hide my underlying feelings of fear, shyness, and not belonging.

These were the residual effects of dealing with my father's drinking and the bullying from childhood. I knew that no matter how successful I became or how many of my dreams came true, I wouldn't be able to have peace until I dealt with my deep hidden wounds and fears. I was an adult, and I couldn't blame anything or anyone from my past for my present life. It was up to me to put out the effort and do something to make things right.

A huge spiritual breakthrough occurred when I began attending a particular Al-Anon meeting in Midtown Manhattan. The meetings were held on Sunday mornings, a challenge for me thanks to my show schedule, which included two performances on Saturday *and* Sunday. To get to the Al-Anon meeting, I had to get up earlier than I would have liked and then leave before the meeting ended to get to the theater on time. It was exhausting, but it was well worth it because it was specifically for adult children of alcoholics, or ACOAs, as we're called. I benefited from all the Al-Anon meetings, but hearing others speak of their experiences growing up in alcoholic households that were so similar to mine had an extra-healing effect and helped to remedy my feelings of isolation.

I had been attending different Al-Anon meetings for a number of years at this point, but whenever there was a group business meeting to elect officers, I would never volunteer, because my schedule was so hectic and I didn't want to take on the three- or six-month commitment that the program quite rightly calls *service*. Sometimes someone would recommend me, but I'd always decline.

At one particular business meeting during the early Sunday morning fellowship, the group asked for someone to volunteer to run the meeting for the next cycle, and before I knew it, my hand was up. I'd had absolutely no intention of taking on the position, but something deep in my soul, something bigger than I was, knew that it was time to trust myself, commit, break through my issues, and do some service. I wasn't sure how I was going to do it, given my show schedule, but I was committed. Sometimes, it turns out, making the commitment is a lot harder than keeping it.

What I thought would be a difficult job wound up changing my perception of many things. One of my new responsibilities was to read welcoming material at the beginning of each meeting. Even though I am an actor, public speaking has never been easy for me. For years, I'd had fantasies of someday becoming a motivational speaker, but reading aloud was one of the things I feared most. I know it makes no sense since I have performed in front of thousands of people and as a kid was often chosen to read aloud. But it's very different when it's just you, without a character or a song to hide behind.

However, I had grown comfortable and felt safe enough with my Sunday morning group to work through my nervousness and do what was needed, and I ended up actually enjoying it.

Another obligation of my position was to find speakers to share their personal experiences at each meeting, which helped me heal more of my childhood shyness, since I had to reach out to people to ask for help and learn to communicate differently. Similar to my fear-based journey with singing in front of people, I was finally having similar breakthroughs with speaking in front of groups of people.

Doing service in Al-Anon took the focus off me and allowed me to be present to help and support the meeting in a loving way without my ego getting involved. Within a couple of weeks of leading the meeting, I felt a new sense of confidence coming over me. I had broken through my fear and felt more emotionally powerful than ever by simply doing service. It felt so good that I started meditating to discover new ways that I could personally incorporate this new perception. Soon I was able to personalize the idea of service and form my own concepts that bled into other aspects of my life and positively shifted my outlook and especially my career. Taken together, meditation, therapy, and Al-Anon helped me to heal deep-rooted wounds and remember just how far I had come on my journey.

CHANGE IS GOOD—RIGHT?

It was around this time that my manager and I decided to part ways. I was beginning to feel that although Renee and I had accomplished many wonderful goals together, we had gone as far as we could in our creative and business relationship. I was thrilled to have recently been approached by the legendary William Morris Agency.

You can't pursue a big agency like William Morris. If they're interested, they'll come to you. One of the senior agents saw me in a benefit performance in a small theater downtown and had his secretary call me to set up a meeting. I'd always dreamed of working with William Morris but was cautious of getting lost in the shuffle of a huge powerful agency, especially when their big stars are their main priority. But on their urging, we agreed to work together on a trial basis without signing a binding agreement. I liked the freedom of not being on contract and being able to exit if things didn't work out, and I was leery of their professed commitment to getting me screen roles. I didn't want a repeat of what had happened years before at J. Michael Bloom. I said my prayers, hoped for the best, and focused on gratitude for being validated by a top talent agency.

Disney asked me to sign on for another year as Mufasa. Given my new outlook, I was delighted to do so. Even though I had been in the show for so many years,

I never took it for granted that Disney would automatically ask me back every year. Colleagues would often say to me, "Disney loves you. You are so lucky. I wish I were in your shoes." But was it luck? My notion was that Disney appreciated me because I showed up on time, kept everything professional, and did my job well. Luck may get you in the door, but it will not sustain you. Only discipline and skill can do that.

As an actor, your work ethic is one of the few things that get you respect and negotiating power come contract time. Being prompt, maintaining consistency, and keeping things simple and free of offstage drama are some of the challenges of doing a long run in a show. It's easy to get bored or distracted by situations at the theater that have nothing to do with the show, but your discipline must be intact to remind you to keep your energy and focus on why you are there.

I am grateful that Disney has always recognized and rewarded performers for their commitment, passion, and previous experience. This was a part of my incentive to continue to strive to excel in the role of Mufasa year after year between contracts.

The new agent, the new contract, and all my new discoveries were life-changing for me, and as much as I loved *The Lion King* and playing Mufasa, I felt a growing need to challenge myself further, especially creatively. My instincts alerted me that some kind of change was coming, but I didn't know what. I'd hoped it would be a TV or film role. I did readings and workshops for new projects, but rarely went to auditions for other shows because I was already playing what I considered the best male role on Broadway. I was the king, after all.

I did audition for the role of Mister in *The Color Purple* because it was too good a part not to consider, and I was starting to feel cautious about being typecast as the good, responsible father; I wanted to prove that I was first and foremost an actor and could play other kinds of characters. There had already been several workshops for the show, but the creative team was holding auditions in New York for their pre-Broadway run in Atlanta. I knew the actor who'd played the role in the workshops would most likely stay with it through its run in NYC. But I still prepared with the material they gave me and had what I thought was quite a good audition. I got positive feedback from the team, but to my disappointment I was not even offered a callback.

Just over a year later, while taking a ten-minute walk home from the gym and within weeks of *The Color Purple* celebrating its first year on Broadway, I got a call to be seen for Mister again, this time for the tour. My first thought was that I was not leaving Broadway to go on the road, so I thanked the casting director for their consideration, told them that I was not interested, and continued my walk home. But as soon as I hung up the phone, I knew that something wasn't right. What was the real reason that I turned down the audition?

I had been asking the universe for a substantial creative challenge, yet I had just turned one down. I had just renewed my contract with Disney, so I really didn't need the job or the money. This allowed me the freedom to use the audition purely as a learning experience and creative outlet.

By the time I got home from the gym I was finally able to admit to myself that I was embarrassed and afraid to go to the audition because of not getting a callback the last time. I was letting my ego get the best of me. I immediately called the casting director back and asked them if I could have the appointment after all, noting that William Morris was now representing me. My primary objective for the audition would be to make myself proud for doing the proper preparation and doing my best while I was in the room. Instead of giving myself the pressure of booking the role, I made it my number one goal to prove to myself that I was still a good actor and could play someone who is so far from who I am in real life.

Preparing the audition material for Mister was difficult, and tapping into my dark emotions and bringing them to the surface was challenging. Mister seemed like the exact opposite of Mufasa, the wise and loving father I'd been playing for nearly five years. Mister was a monster. I left the audition thinking I had succeeded in reaching my goal, and I didn't care at all about getting a callback this time. I was satisfied that I had done the necessary work and preparation.

A few days later I got a call from William Morris about a callback for the show. I was flattered to hear this, but didn't understand why my agents would think I would even consider going. Part of our agreement in working together was to focus on TV and film. Since parting ways with Renee, I was no longer paying anyone a commission for my work in *The Lion King*, and I enjoyed saving and investing the extra money. Why would anyone think I'd give that up to go on tour?

After a lot of back and forth, William Morris asked me to please go to the callback as a favor to them. This seemed very strange to me, but I went. The day after my callback, I was made an offer—not for the tour, but to take over the role of Mister on Broadway instead. I was elated! I had asked the universe for a big challenge, and I had gotten one. I was able to meet it by focusing on the work and not the result. This was new territory for me, so I was sincerely surprised to have booked a terrific job in the process of challenging myself in this way.

I'd often wondered what it would take for me to leave *The Lion King*, which I still loved so much. Well, leaving to be a principal in another hit show on Broadway felt like the perfect practical move.

I was excited to have this new opportunity, but unfortunately, my negotiations for *The Color Purple* were not easy, and the offer was not as lucrative as I had hoped. Accepting the contract would mean taking a substantial cut in pay, plus, once again, paying an agent's commission. I reminded William Morris that my focus was still on breaking into TV and film and that I hoped that since I would now be playing such a dramatic character (not to mention a human being for the first time in a while) that they would feel more confident about setting up meetings for me with casting directors for TV and film. I may have mentioned that there was a lot at stake for me leaving the security of a steady paycheck in a certified hit show. They assured me that taking the role would be a good move in that direction. Above all else, at that time I really needed the spiritual and mental challenge of taking the creative journey to craft my own version of Mister more than the money I wished I would earn.

So, I set up a meeting at the Disney offices with Todd Lacy, *The Lion King*'s lovely and supportive associate producer, to thank him for my extraordinary journey with the show and to give him my four weeks' notice. Disney had been incredible to me, so I thought it best and most respectful to break my bittersweet news in person. When I told Todd that I would be leaving, he seemed shocked and kept asking me if I was really leaving for good, which was a bit of a surprise. Looking back on it, I probably could have asked for, and gotten, a leave of absence to take on *The Color Purple* and eventually return. But I figured it was someone else's turn to play Mufasa. I just assumed that after *The Color Purple* closed, I would take up the gypsy life again, hopefully with a serious new emphasis on TV and film work.

On my last day at *The Lion King*, I had fragrant potted flowers delivered to the producers at the office and to every department at the theater. I wanted to leave on a high note and put smiles on everyone's faces. It was important for me to let them know how much I had valued our relationships over the years and how much I would miss them while demonstrating to the all-knowing universe how grateful I was for always providing me with powerful instincts and new ways to express myself.

THEY CALL ME *MISTER* WHITE

My research for Mister began with the source, Alice Walker's novel, which was not only a runaway best seller, but had also won both the Pulitzer Prize and the National Book Award for Fiction. I had seen the movie many times, but never read the book. In the film and in the script of the show, Mister seemed to be constantly angry, and I knew that there had to be more to him. Why was he so heated? How could a character that seemed to be the boss of nearly everyone around him always be so mad? What was at the root of his rage?

As I suspected, the book did not present Mister as merely a stock mean guy. In the novel, I saw Mister as a hurt, lost man-child who is trapped between the kind of life that he wants and the kind of life that is expected of him. His father, Old Mister, wants to pass on to him the legacy and responsibilities of the land that he has acquired where he was once a slave. But Mister wants more freedom, the kind of freedom his son Harpo is afforded because of the social changes of the time and difference between the generations. The key scene for me is when Old Mister comes to the house and tells Mister to put his girlfriend and true love, the ever-flirtatious Shug Avery, out of his house, where she is staying with him and his wife, Celie, and their kids.

Mister becomes like a little hurt boy again, rebelling against his father's wishes. Everyone perceives Mister as a powerful man, yet spiritually he is powerless until he is able to make peace with everyone in his life, himself included.

For a very demanding three weeks, I was blessed with rehearsing the role of the troubled, tortured Mister during the day, while performing the role of the wise, benevolent father Mufasa in the evenings. Being a part of two incredible Broadway shows at the same time is a thrill that I will never forget. A major gift and surprise on my journey playing Mister was even deeper healing regarding my own father.

Researching Mister and black men like him who were born and raised during the early part of the 1900s, I gained a new level of respect, compassion, and appreciation for what so many men of color had to endure coming out of slavery and adjusting to a new world. Some adapted well and were strong, but others had more difficulty adjusting. These kinds of discoveries helped me remember many of my father's good qualities, traits I had probably forgotten because of my own childhood pain and judgment. I was beginning to see my late father as not only an unpredictable alcoholic, but also as a man who took his responsibilities to heart and did the very best he could under his circumstances. This growing compassion helped me remember positive aspects of him that I had long ago erased from memory.

There was a bit of doubt from some of my *Purple* colleagues regarding my approach, but my choice to uncover the hurt and trapped aspects of Mister instead of limiting myself to his overt meanness was a gamble that paid off richly. Many women, especially black women, have a special kinship with *The Color Purple*. And the most frequent compliments I received at the stage door were from women telling me that they had never even considered that Mister's anger masked great sadness and personal misery, and that by the end of the play they wanted both him and the long-suffering Celie to have peace.

I have two wonderful memories of my year and a half performing in *The Color Purple*. Once, on the stage after a performance—soon after Fantasia Barrino from *American Idol* had taken over the role of Celie—Oprah Winfrey, one of the producers of the show, told me that she thought I was magnificent in the role of Mister. We hugged and then took a picture together, a copy of which is framed in nearly all of my relatives' homes. All that

I could think at the time was, "At this moment, Oprah Winfrey knows who I am." She may have forgotten as soon as she turned away, but at that very moment I was on her radar and had her attention.

The other great memory came after a matinee, when I went out into the lobby still dressed as Mister to collect for Broadway Cares/Equity Fights AIDS and saw Thomas Schumacher, the president of Disney Theatrical Group, coming down from the balcony with a group of students. He hugged and congratulated me and later sent me a wonderful handwritten note telling me how proud of me he was.

But not everything was coming up roses, at least not without some heavy gardening on my part. During my run in *The Color Purple*, William Morris sent me on fewer than ten on-camera auditions, and I felt like I was back where I'd started, except that now I was making a lot less money. I offered to put myself on tape or come into the office with prepared scenes or monologues—anything to get William Morris to promote me beyond theater.

I was feeling as frustrated as I had with J. Michael Bloom. I got a call directly from a casting director about a new film called *The Invention of Lying*, which was to be the directorial debut of Ricky Gervais, who cowrote the script. When I booked it, my agents asked me why I hadn't had them negotiate my contract. I reminded them yet again that I was serious about broadening my career beyond theater. Since I had booked it on my own, all future residuals would come to me. I was no longer willing to give away money that only *I* was working hard for. My instincts were telling me that as much as I'd hoped things would work out with William Morris, they too had pigeonholed me as a theater actor, and my days with them were probably numbered.

The movie shot in Lowell, Massachusetts, a quaint town just outside of Boston. They sent me by train the night before and put me up in a lovely hotel. I filmed my scenes the next day, my birthday, April 10. After my scenes were wrapped, Ricky Gervais presented me with a birthday cake, full of lit candles, and the whole crew sang "Happy Birthday" to me. It was extremely thoughtful, because I hadn't even told anyone it was my birthday.

After my first movie experience, I resumed the role of a Broadway gypsy once again, generally unemployed with the exception of a short gig here and there. Fortunately, I had saved and invested a decent amount of money but, unfortunately, was now even more reliant on William Morris coming through with on-camera work, which did not materialize. My instincts felt even stronger that my so-called agents were not working as hard as I thought they could on my behalf.

I prayed for a sign that my feelings were right, and soon after, I got a call out of the blue from the casting directors at *Law & Order*, of which I had done three episodes many years before. The call wasn't for me to audition, but to offer me the role of a bailiff for two episodes, meaning more on-camera time and future residuals. This was just the sign that I needed. I was doing better by myself than my big-deal agency was doing.

Months passed with still very few auditions from my agents, and almost all of them were for stage musicals. As I'd done with J. Michael Bloom years before, I asked William Morris if it might be best that we part ways. They assured me that they were doing all that they could, and that I should hang on longer, but my instincts were usually right, and those instincts were telling me differently.

The tipping point came when Disney called to ask about my interest in opening *The Lion King* in Las Vegas. I was thrilled! Since parting ways with Renee, I had been negotiating my own contracts with Disney directly and quite comfortably. Another thing that I had made perfectly clear to William Morris before we began working together was that my previous relationships and contracts were my own, especially regarding Disney and *The Lion King*. Disney was like family to me. They were generous and fair with my contracts, and I didn't need any outside "help" poking around in our great relationship. William Morris thought they could get me a better deal than I was getting. I doubted it, but I let them try. What they came back with was no improvement. I thanked them for trying and told them that I would take it from there. But they persisted.

After a lot of give and take, I offered to give them a

onetime payment for their efforts, purely as a courtesy. They became insistent and told me they expected me to pay them a commission on the full length of my upcoming contract, which they had not negotiated, purely because I had allowed them to make a call. I was dumbfounded at such nerve and their feeling of entitlement. Money isn't everything, but money earned performing eight shows a week, week after week, is extremely hard-earned. If you don't put value on your time and talent, no one else will.

When I left *The Lion King*, I trusted William Morris to help me expand my career and my growing brand, but they could not—or would not—hold up their end of the deal. This was the last of many straws. I reminded them that when we had first started working together, I'd asked to sign a contract, but they had "suggested" that we keep it on a freelance basis, so actually I owed them nothing. I thanked them for their efforts the past two years and made it clear that I thought it best that we part ways.

On the same day I settled my self-negotiated new contract with Disney, I received more great news. After going on dozens of commercial auditions over the past few months and getting close, I booked a national commercial for FedEx that flew me out to L.A. to film. It felt like a gift from the universe for taking leaps of faith, dealing with the disappointments along the way, and trusting my instincts enough to act on them. I couldn't have been more excited to reapproach Mufasa with a few more years of wisdom and maturity under my belt—and to have a new adventure in my childhood fantasy destination. *Viva Las Vegas*!

Whether or not "showbiz" is how you earn your living and pay for your life, it is vital to learn how to manage your time, your talent, and your finances. The goal may not always be to make the most money. There may be instances, especially in the arts, where taking less money for a job may be a better overall decision regarding a role or prospect that is more self-fulfilling or more important in building your career. These are all business decisions, and having savings, making financial investments, and planning your money management wisely can afford you the opportunity to make those choices more freely. It is imperative that you put value on what you have to offer, because your talent is one of your most vital business assets.

When you're in the arts or in show business, it's easy to forget that you are, in fact, in business. As an actor, whether you are incorporated or not (and yes, you should be), you are not only the commodity but the CEO, too. Staying on top of your business can help you determine what your next step needs to be and when to take it. This will help you in your decision-making and continuing to move forward with your spirit and reputation intact. As in any business, there is never a reason to behave like an entitled jerk, but don't sell yourself short, either. Everyone on your team—your agent, manager, etc.—works for you. They are not doing you a favor when they submit you for projects or advise you about employment. It is their job to work with and for you and your best interests—and you mustn't ever relinquish the power of your position out of any sense of fear, guilt, or unrealistic obligation. You must always remember that they are working with you in a group effort to craft your career.

One of the best business and personal decisions you can make is to balance your professional life with service, which can expand your sense of self and your productivity, as well as energize you in ways you might never suspect. Spiritual leaders from the beginning of recorded history have made note of the role of service as a tool to enlightenment. But it works in the professional arena, too, which is not terribly surprising, because— if you're doing it right—there's an intimate relationship between who you are and what you do for a living.

There are two kinds of service. One is what we might think of as volunteering—doing things for other people and taking the focus off ourselves. It's a paradox of life that we find ourselves when we are most willing to lose ourselves, though service is not about loss. It's all about gain. Not only do those who receive our service benefit, but we do as well. Service is the single best way we can put gratitude to work, to transform our thoughts and feelings into action.

The other way to put service into action in your life is to redefine activities, particularly burdensome activities, as service rather than labor. Labor sounds difficult, uninteresting, and unpleasant, whereas service is elevating. It is self-fulfilling in the best way and helps us experience our work more as an opportunity (if not a pure joy) than a penalty we pay for the privilege of living. As an actor, potential boredom of constant repetition—the same lines and moves eight times a week for protracted periods of time—can be a problem if you think of performing as a job that you do for compensation.

If, on the other hand, you embrace the idea that the performance has nothing to do with you, but everything to do with the audience, your fellow performers, the whole company together, and even the playwright, then you are much more likely to give your performance your best possible effort. It's extremely gratifying to please other people, and doing it cannot help but make us think better of ourselves and our professions, and to move through life with even more confidence and self-esteem. Service is ultimate nourishment for the head, heart, and spirit.

FOOD FOR THOUGHT

1. What are the long-term benefits of delaying gratification in the professional and personal areas of your life? Is there a right time and place to move forward, stay put, or retreat?

2. How can the lessons of our professional lives help us confront family tragedies and other personal losses?

3. Have you ever had such a compelling intuitive feeling that it almost felt like a message from the universe, or some form of ESP? What did you do?

4. Whom in your life do you need to forgive—a parent, sibling, child, partner, colleague . . . or yourself?

5. How important to you are service, volunteerism, and "giving back"? What do you think the benefits might be of expanding your participation even more? How can these activities teach you even more about yourself?

6. Have you ever considered therapy? If so, and you committed to it, how was it for you? If not, why not? Do you secretly think that there is something wrong with asking for help when it comes to your emotional and psychological health?

7. How does playing the blame game hurt us more than those we point our fingers at?

8. What is your reaction to the phrase "It's never too late"? Do you believe it? Think it's untrue? What would you do if you really believed that it's never too late?

Find yourself by losing yourself in the service of others.

—Herman Harrell Horne,
educational philosopher

Chapter 13

NEW WAYS TO ROAR . . . AND PURR

As any actor can tell you, constant rejection can wreak havoc on your spirit. You need an abundance of courage, patience, and confidence to turn big dreams into realities. The talents that you possess are unique and unlike anything that any other person on the planet has to offer, and your faith in them will be tested throughout your life and career. When overcome with doubt, your passion to share your gifts must outweigh your fear every time, making it that much more important to acquire nurturing tools to help you maintain your mental and physical stamina. Practices like meditation for stillness and clarity, psychotherapy for maintaining positive mental health, and yoga for spiritual and physical balance and strength can counterbalance inevitable setbacks. Engaging in these spiritual practices can help replenish your well of optimism and help you nourish your spirit, as well as your dreams.

I wanted to live differently in Las Vegas than I had in Manhattan, so before I got there, I began to envision what would be my dream apartment. I was blessed to live in a gorgeous Harlem brownstone in New York, but I had always wanted to experience living in a loft space with huge windows. When I got to Vegas, that's exactly what I found. The loft was a modern industrial corner unit near downtown. It was on the twenty-second floor with windows to the ceiling and spectacular views of the Strip and the mountains beyond. It had a huge stainless steel chef's kitchen with a portable island, and the building had a gym and a rooftop pool.

I also purchased a car for the first time in twenty years and enjoyed exploring what kind of car fit my personality at that time of my life. I settled on a midsize athletic SUV that sat up nice and high, but wasn't too large or imposing.

Rehearsals for the Vegas company of *The Lion King* almost felt like starting over again, because a majority of the cast had never done the show before. The librettists, Irene Mecchi and Roger Allers, were also on hand to tinker with the book for the first time in many years. So, there were lots of table reads where we analyzed the scenes, dialogue, and relationships among the characters. In the end, the show was shortened a bit, and the team was so happy with the changes that they eventually instituted them in all the productions being staged around the world.

The original Vegas company opened at Mandalay Bay Resort on May 15, 2009, to fantastic reviews. Although the show had been on tour for many years, it had never played Las Vegas, and the town ate it up. Because of my love of variety shows as a kid—and before I'd ever even heard of Broadway—my childhood showbiz fantasies usually involved being on TV or singing in a show on the Vegas Strip. And now I was doing just that!

It was also in Vegas that I had my second experience with Bikram yoga. My only previous Bikram practice had been seven years before in Denver with Michelle Camaya, a cast member I'd worked with on the Gazelle Tour. She knew that spirituality was important to me and suggested that I try Bikram for its balance and meditation benefits. I was instantly hesitant when she told me that Bikram is a form of "hot yoga" and that the ninety-minute practice would be in a room heated to approximately 105 degrees. I hated extreme heat and humidity, but she was the one teaching, and I trusted her enough to give it a try.

I was in good physical shape from working out at the gym and thought the poses would be easy. Not so! It was the hardest, longest ninety minutes I had ever experienced. There were moments that I thought I would pass out because I was treating the class like a competitive workout instead of a moving meditation. Throughout the practice, I'd look around and wonder why no one was fainting or running out of the door for cool air.

It was like being in a dream where everyone else is calm and collected and I alone am suffering. It hurt my body, my feelings, and my ego.

When the class finally ended, I got out of there as fast as I could, grabbed my things, and raced toward the door. Some other members of the cast who were in class invited me to join them for lunch, but I made up an excuse so I could get back to my place and collect my nerves.

When I got to my apartment, I nearly collapsed. My head was spinning trying to figure out what had just happened and how awful it felt. I wondered why on earth Michelle thought I'd like it. After my breathing settled, strange sensations began to move through me. My body and my head started to tingle. I felt a sort of weightlessness, like my body was expanding and taking in oxygen differently. It felt almost euphoric. I couldn't believe that less than an hour before, I'd felt like I was falling apart, yet now I was in a strange kind of ecstasy. It was an amazing and surprising feeling that both excited and frightened me.

My instincts told me that I needed to take up the practice and explore the journey of suffering to enlightenment ASAP, but I was honest enough with myself to know that I wasn't yet mentally prepared for the overall changes it would bring to my life, nor the responsibilities that would come with it. I was not ready to let go of my present attachments and way of life, which I assumed would shift drastically—and I sensed all of this in an instant.

Unfortunately, I spent the next seven years making every excuse I could not to go back to the practice. As with most things that we try to avoid, the reality of it never leaves you. All the years in between, no matter how good my life was, I knew in the back of my mind that I was avoiding something vital that was good and nurturing. I swore to myself that if Michelle was cast in the Vegas company and still teaching this form of yoga, I would sign up and try to take it on.

Thankfully she was, and as soon as previews were done and the show officially opened, I dove in, sometimes taking as many as five classes a week. My body took to the heat surprisingly fast, and very quickly Bikram yoga became my ninety-minute moving meditation, a special time for me to relax, regain flexibility, and re-center. All these years later, I still practice a minimum of three times a week no matter where I am.

The positive effects of practicing Bikram had an effect that was similar to how Al-Anon and the idea of service affected me: I was able to extend the physical, mental, and spiritual flexibility I was attaining in Bikram into other areas of my life. Instead of running around and creating busyness for myself before each show, I began to spend most days attending a Bikram practice, then driving forty-five minutes from the Strip to the healing mountains of Red Rock Canyon or Mount Charleston to meditate and listen to the wind. I was discovering even more new and important ways to nurture and replenish my spirit, and they had positive effects on my health, sleep, diet, and attitude.

While I was performing in Vegas, Disney invited me to be a part of the very first D23, a huge Disney fan event held in and around Disneyland and Disney California Adventure in Anaheim, California. I sang "They Live in You" backed by a local choir and afterward was invited to dinner at the fabulous Napa Rose at Disney's California Adventure park with members of the team that created the original animated *Lion King* feature. It was fascinating to listen in on their shared stories and inspirations for the blockbuster whose success no one could have possibly predicted. On another occasion, I had the tremendous honor of being flown to Los Angeles to sing "They Live in You" at Roy E. Disney's memorial at the El Capitan Theatre in Hollywood. The tribute to Walt's nephew, who had dedicated his life to Disney animation, was beautiful and emotional. David A. Bossert's book *Remembering Roy E. Disney* ends with a recounting of this performance. "They Live in You" was one of Roy's favorite songs, if not his very favorite. I performed it with a local children's choir. The performance closed out the ceremony. I barely made it to the end of the song without breaking down.

I loved my new life in Vegas with my great apartment, Bikram practice, meditative drives, and the open desert landscape just outside the city. But after nearly a year there, my instincts started hinting that another change was imminent. I thought they were suggesting that my next move might be to spend more time on the West Coast and even resettle in Los Angeles to pursue TV and film full-time.

I visited L.A. and other parts of California often when I was living in Las Vegas. A lot of time had passed since my disastrous monthlong encounter with the City of Angels many years before. Now, I was more mature and open to what might be awaiting me in the city and its surrounding environs. I meditated more about moving to the West Coast, but at night I would dream about being back in New York City. The more I meditated, the more I began to miss the culture and cosmopolitanism of New York—but there was no way I was going to leave *The Lion King* and go back to being an unemployed gypsy making the rounds of Broadway auditions.

I focused my prayers and Bikram practice on remaining open to create space for whatever possibilities the universe had in store for me next. I practiced acceptance and gratefully reminded myself that I had a choice in any opportunity that came my way.

Then, out of the clear blue, I got a call from Disney asking if I would be interested in returning to Broadway. Just like that, I was heading back to Manhattan. I worried about maintaining the peaceful lifestyle I'd created for myself in Nevada. New York is the most amazing city in the world for many reasons. It's a place of countless options, but it's also a place of extremes, and you can find yourself having the best and worst day of your life all on the same day. I needed to go back to NYC with a solid positive foundation that I could tap into so that I wouldn't be pulled into the stressful hustle and bustle of the city.

My solutions were to research a few Bikram studios in the city before I went back and to ship my car there so I could get out of the city at a moment's notice and get myself back to nature. After just under a year of *Viva Las Vegas*, and having discovered many life-altering nurturing tools for myself, I headed back to the Big Apple.

BACK TO BROADWAY

After leaving Las Vegas, I had just over a month back in New York to reacclimate and rest, allowing me time to settle into my Bikram practice at a new yoga studio and pack up my car for a meditative ten-hour road trip to spend some quality time with my family in Cincinnati. About a week before rehearsals began, I had the honor of performing "They Live in You" at a tribute for Julie Taymor, who was being honored by New Dramatists with their 2010 Lifetime Achievement Award. It was a wonderful reintro back to the Broadway-theater scene and an honor in itself to be a part of such a wonderful celebration of Julie's many talents and contributions.

Going back into the Broadway company of *The Lion King* was another great adventure. I had been away for a couple of years, and there were lots of cast members I didn't know, including several new principals who were starting when I was. Since the creative team was so pleased with the new, tightened Vegas version they'd created, those changes were being put into the Broadway production at the time. We rehearsed as a full company, which helped us bond and made it almost feel like a new production.

After I had gotten back into the swing of *The Lion King*'s eight-times-a-week performance schedule at the Minskoff Theatre, Disney invited me to be a part of another prestigious event at the *New York Times* 10th Annual Arts & Leisure Weekend. My event was "Sir Tim Rice & Friends," an amazing evening featuring the reigning lord of Broadway lyricists, of course, and seven Broadway performers paying tribute to the Oscar- and Tony-winning Sir Tim and to scores of Disney shows, both past and present. I was honored that Disney gave me the opportunity to be featured as a soloist with songs from shows besides *The Lion King*—like *Mary Poppins*, *The Little Mermaid*, and *King David*. It was a fortunate creative outlet for me. I was able to show aspects of my talent that differ from those I display in my role as King Mufasa.

Another childhood dream came true that led to yet another when Disney then offered me the opportunity to perform my own show as a headliner on a Disney cruise that sailed the Atlantic for six days from Florida to Portugal. I was a huge fan of *The Love Boat* when I was growing up and would watch it religiously every week. It was like a variety show where I'd get to see a different selection of my favorite stars in each episode. I had always dreamed of performing on a cruise ship, but never wanted to commit to the minimum six-month contract you have to sign to do it. Plus, the working conditions are often less than glamorous, to say the least. But the Disney offer was ideal because my only obligation was to perform two solo shows and offer a Q and A with the audience. The rest of the time, I would be free to enjoy the cruise and the wonderful adventures on board and at the ports of call. Oh, and my stateroom was magnificent!

My show was put together by the supremely talented Jeff Lee, who had directed me in *The Lion King* tour as well as the *New York Times* tribute event. It was sort of a one-man version of the Sir Tim Rice concert, with me performing both male and female songs from the Disney catalog: everything from Radames's "Fortune Favors the Brave" from *Aida* to Ariel's "Part of Your World" from *The Little Mermaid*. I was admittedly a little concerned with how die-hard Disney fans would react to my singing some of them, but it was so well received that I was inspired to approach Thomas Schumacher, the president of Disney Theatrical Group and the producer of all its shows, about recording a CD of Disney classics with new, more personal arrangements of my own. Being the amazing person that he is, and the best and most approachable boss anyone could ever have, he made time for me.

I was at a point in my career where I needed to record a Broadway-style CD. When I'd do singing engagements, people would frequently ask me if I had a CD. They wanted to hear more, but the only music I had on the market was dance music, which I love, but which I'd written and recorded many years before. I needed something to represent my more theatrical vocal skills but didn't want to record the same standard Broadway songs that a lot of performers chose. Tom gave me his blessing, along with access to the entire Disney musical catalog. After a lot of listening, I narrowed it down to Disney on Broadway tunes. After settling on thirteen songs, I negotiated the rights with Disney's legal reps. Next, I needed a skilled and versatile musical director and musician to collaborate with me. I immediately thought of Jim Abbott.

Jim, who is as likable and patient as he is talented, was already in the Disney family, having done the dance arrangements and played in the orchestra for *Aida*. He had also served as music director and conductor for *Tarzan*. I had worked with him briefly on another recording for Disney, and he had been the musical director for the Tim Rice event. I felt a great creative vibe with him right from the beginning. I thought he'd be too busy, but when I asked, he said yes—as long as we made it fun!

The two us got together to create some new arrangements for voice and piano. We both wanted the record to have a "live" feel, so he gathered some of the best musicians in New York to do a couple of jam sessions until we came up with the kind of sound we wanted. From there, we went to a studio in Long Island City to record the music with a full orchestra, while I recorded the final vocals over two days at a studio in Midtown Manhattan. It was beyond fun, and the time went way too fast.

Making the record allowed me to perceive my job at *The Lion King* from a different perspective. The process of planning, rehearsing, and putting the record together broke the monotony of performing eight shows a week, because the show was now financing my new artistic endeavors, which in turn energized me and helped to reinvigorate my performances.

Before I knew it, we were done, and the CD was finished, packaged, and ready for sale. *Disney My Way* was released on October 12, 2012, to excellent reviews, thankfully. I was grateful for having the means to finance and invest in my dream. Of all of the goals I've accomplished so far, with the exception of my record-breaking run as Mufasa, my *Disney My Way* CD is what I am most proud of. The release concert a few weeks later was held at what was then the recently opened 54 Below. I could not have been happier when

I saw Mr. Thomas Schumacher sitting front and center and cheering me on like a proud papa. (Although everyone in the business calls him Tom, I continue to call him Thomas as a sign of respect, and adding *Mr.* is a sign of my gratitude.)

One of the many major lessons I have learned working for Disney all these years is to never ever underestimate your product or take it for granted. *The Lion King* is the highest grossing show in Broadway history, but Disney still advertises and does press as if it opened just yesterday.

During one press event, I had a conversation with Dennis Crowley, Disney Theatrical Group's public relations chief. (You may remember this conversation from chapter 1!) We realized that after twelve years with *The Lion King* on Broadway, on tour, and in Las Vegas, my four thousandth performance as King Mufasa was fast approaching. I hadn't been keeping track at all; to me, performing in an amazing hit show as a character I was extremely proud to play was icing on the cake. After the day's interviews concluded, Dennis brought the subject up again and shared with me that in his many years of doing press for dozens of Broadway shows, he had rarely witnessed what I had accomplished. He encouraged me to acknowledge the occasion in some way—which is, of course, just what I did.

Even as I considered and planned for my celebration, I could feel another change brewing like a weather front on my ever-shifting horizon. I loved my life and my schedule, no matter how rigorous and repetitive, but I began to feel a desire to live differently. I didn't know what that would look like, but I strongly sensed impending change. I wanted to do service besides performing; things like writing, public speaking, and possibly teaching.

As Mufasa, I had a long break during act 2, when I had the dressing room all to myself. So, I started using that time to write about my feelings, experiences, and observations about show business. I began to write down my thoughts about mastering the challenges of daily repetition and maintaining a consistently high level of performance over the long haul. Part of what had supported me and allowed me to continue to progress in *The Lion King* for all those years had been learning different ways along my path of finding a balance between my hectic, repetitive schedule on the one hand, and learning to trust myself enough to allow room for spontaneity and self-nurturing on the other. The balance was constantly shifting, causing me to be present and aware of my feelings and my relationships to my work and to myself.

The more that I wrote about my experiences and reflected on parts of my life that I'd been missing for so many years, the further my instincts were triggered that it might be time for a major transition. In the past, this would have made me fearful and sad, but now I felt hopeful.

At first I thought I'd wait until the beginning of the

year to see if I'd be asked to renew my contract as Mufasa. But then I realized that the most powerful position I could take would be to make the choice myself. If I waited, Disney might make me an offer that would be too difficult to refuse, and the temptation to ignore my gut feeling would be too great. In addition, as much as I loved playing Mufasa, I dreaded even the thought of ever overstaying my welcome. No one wants to stay too long at the party, even if it's the best one you've ever attended. I was certain of how I felt, and my instincts were telling me that it was time to take another leap of faith to create openings for new kinds of life and service.

I scheduled a meeting with Mr. Thomas Schumacher for September 24, 2014, a month after my four thousandth performance—late enough in the afternoon that I could catch a monumentally entertaining matinee of *Aladdin,* then and still playing at the New Amsterdam. I wanted to thank this good man and excellent employer in person for so many wonderful years, and to inform him that it was time for me to get off the most amazing ride I'd ever taken.

It was time for someone else to become the king. I told him I was in no rush to go, and that I would stay until my contract ran out in June of 2015, but that it was time to move on. This would give Disney a full nine months to recast Mufasa and for me to birth some fresh ideas about investigating the new life I knew was waiting for me. I felt a tremendous sense of gratitude and accomplishment after giving my notice. I would miss the show and my *Lion King* family, but I had faith that I would always be a part of the wonderful Disney family. As a matter of fact, soon after announcing that I would be leaving, Disney offered me extraordinary performance gigs that would take me around the world for the next year and beyond.

I was proud to have found the clarity and faith to trust my instincts and to choose to make space to receive new opportunities for serving and sharing. It energized me further, and much to my surprise, writing became a passion—which is why you are getting to hold this book in your hands. Now, I'm talking about someone who never learned to type and who "hunts and pecks."

But I still found it healing to spend time organizing my thoughts and putting them into words. It became both a meditation and therapy for me. When I was writing, I completely lost track of time. I felt a cleansing relief afterward when I looked back at what I'd typed, and I would be absolutely amazed at how much I'd done. After writing a substantial amount, I took the vulnerable step of sharing it with a few friends in various fields, people whose opinions I trusted. Much to my relief, their feedback was unanimously positive. They all encouraged me to keep writing.

I remembered that Thomas Schumacher had written a book a few years back titled *How Does the Show Go On? An Introduction to the Theater*. After reading it, I asked him for a meeting to talk about his process of putting it all together. We discussed the kinds of messages that I wanted to share, and he thought it was a great idea. I gave him some of my writings, and without my even having to ask, he immediately offered to help me.

With his generous assistance and encouragement, I crafted a foundation that led to finding a literary agent who in turn assisted in my getting a book deal! I'd like to say that it was another dream come true, except that I'd never had the dream of writing a book. This was beyond anything that I ever expected and a true sign from the universe that it was indeed time to spread my wings and do other things—hopefully to touch and inspire people in different ways.

No one was more surprised than I was that a writer was living somewhere inside of me. I credit my yoga practice and various forms of meditation for helping me release, let go, and allow other parts of myself to shine through. We are all full of endless potential, and it is vital to find tools that assist in making space for them to be revealed.

I spent the months leading up to my final show writing away and experimenting to see what kind of life I'd like to have after I left *The Lion King*. Travel and reestablishing and updating friendships were at the top of my list. While doing eight shows a week for so many years, I'd lost touch with friends who had stopped inviting me to gatherings because I would invariably decline due to my hectic schedule, especially on the weekends.

I made a conscious effort to adjust my routines and get back on those social lists, because I realized that community outside of the business is essential. In addition, I sought out and accepted any and every opportunity for upcoming work that involved travel, including an offer from Disney Cruise Line to perform my solo *Disney My Way* show on a two-week northern European cruise that sailed a few days after what would be my final *Lion King* performance. It was the perfect way to close a wonderful chapter and begin my new journey toward a new life!

As the date of my last performance approached, friends and family came from all over the world to support me and see me in the show. When the very last day arrived, I sat in my dressing room reminiscing about my unbelievable thirteen-year journey with *The Lion King* and what a tremendous blessing it's been to have this wonderful vehicle as a foundation to incorporate so many of my life lessons and growth.

While playing King Mufasa, I matured from my late thirties to my early fifties, and playing the iconic king and father helped me tap into and develop a strong leader in myself and heal old wounds. It also allowed me to find deeper forgiveness and even gratitude for my own father while drawing me closer to my family, all while exercising my passion for performing.

During intermission of my final performance on July

5, 2015, Disney had yet another surprise for me up their sleeve. Stage Management knocked on my door and handed me a pile of flyers that Disney had stuffed into every playbill. It was my favorite picture taken of me as Mufasa, and on it was written THE LION KING AND DISNEY THEATRICAL PRODUCTIONS CONGRATULATE ALTON FITZGERALD WHITE, BROADWAY'S LONGEST RUNNING MUFASA, ON HIS 4,308TH PERFORMANCE WITH THE LION KING. "Your passion and talent will be missed, but you will always be a part of our pride."

Of all the emotions I've discussed in this book, at the top of that list is gratitude. It is such a simple characteristic that it's easy to forget; however, remembering to acknowledge it can instantly change your perception of everything in your life.

No matter how hard you strive to make your dreams come true, dealing with setbacks that leave you drained and frustrated, you must never believe that you are entitled or that the universe owes you anything. Entitlement is the opposite of gratitude, and surrendering to the illusion that life owes you something will not get you where you want to go. Gratitude prompts you to be appreciative for being blessed with unique abilities, talents, and gifts. It makes you thankful to have been given something special to be passionate about and to share with the world. Deep, sincere appreciation must embody all that you work diligently for and should always be a dominant characteristic at your foundation, reminding you why you are pursuing your passion in the first place.

When every other tool that I have mentioned in this book has been exhausted, gratitude will remain, no matter what challenge you are facing. It will humble you, help you focus to re-center yourself, and bring you back to your true intentions, which is to simply share your talent and gifts. I did not reach 4,308 performances as King Mufasa in The Lion King *by counting and keeping score, but because my focus was most often grounded in gratitude for the gift of being a working actor.*

FOOD FOR THOUGHT

1. What are the ways you nourish (rather than just feed) your body, mind, and spirit—and what are the ways you keep them in balance with your life and work? Are there arenas you mean to explore but keep from yourself?

2. Are you avoiding things in your life that you know you eventually have to confront? How does avoidance block us and keep us from contentment and personal fulfillment?

3. How does having a balanced physical, emotion, and spiritual life help when times are tough? How does it help when times are good and everything in your life is just as you wished or imagined it could be?

4. How can you help turn a fear of impending transitions in your life into hope and eager anticipation?

5. What is the role of gratitude in your life, and what are its gifts?

All beautiful art, all great art belongs here: the essence of both is gratitude.

—Friedrich Nietzsche, philosopher

As we express our gratitude, we must never forget that the highest appreciation is not to utter words, but to live by them.

—John Fitzgerald Kennedy

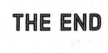

THE END

Acknowledgments

Yvans Jourdain, Rashid Ferrod Davis, Marty Jones, Louise Bernikow, Andra Ward, Anthony Hollins, Ricky Gervais, Josh Tower, Beverly Harpenau, Darrell Miller, Donald Lawrence, Jennifer Beckman Longenecker, Nancy Allen, Bruce Stegman, Tajma Beverly, Jack Louiso, David Stull, Garth Drabinsky, Lynette DuPree, Tina Fabrique, Kimberly JuJuan, Rufus Bonds Jr., Brian Chandler, Henry Menendez, Hinton Battle, Bob Avian, Vinnie Liff, Ben Harney, Mitchel Lemsky, Alan Savage, Ken Hanson, Renee Harriston, Julie Taymor, Doyle Newmyer, Robyn Newmyer, Kenny Ingram, Lelund Durond Thompson, Rockell Metcalf, Rosa Curry, Jim Abbott, Lori Abbott, Diane Hancock, Dennis Crowley, Jeff Lee, Ryan Murphy, Cameron Mackintosh, Garth Drabinsky, Pam Young, Josette Williams, Todd Lacy, Winnie Ho, Monica Vasquez, Robbie Todd, Arlene Goldberg, Pamela Bradshaw, Jay Hatcher, Charlie Hall, Georgio Rodriguez, Ron Werner, Adam Dworkin, Christopher Camp, Ron Vodicka, Pixie Esmonde,

Ruthlyn Salomans, Gregory Miller, Thomas Schlenk, and James Brown Orleans.

Richard Curtis, my literary agent, who helped to make this book happen, and master editors Michael Lassell and Wendy Lefkon, who have been absolute dreams to work with. I cannot thank The Universe enough for your patience, passion, and expertise and for discovering a new spiritual brother and sister in both of you!

And last, but certainly not least, Mr. Thomas Schumacher, who is truly one of the most brilliant and kind human beings that I know. You, sir, are a fine example of using your many wonderful gifts to be of service to others, as you have so often done for me!